Teacher's Book

Business Studies:
A CORE CURRICULUM

IAN DORTON AND ALEX SMITH

Hodder & Stoughton
A MEMBER OF THE HODDER HEADLINE GROUP

Orders: please contact Bookpoint Ltd, 39 Milton Park, Abingdon, Oxon OX14 4TD. Telephone: (44) 01235 400414, Fax: (44) 01235 400454. Lines are open from 9.00–6.00, Monday to Saturday, with a 24-hour message answering service. Email address: orders@bookpoint.co.uk

A catalogue record for this title is available from The British Library

ISBN 0 340 730 439

First published 1999
Impression number   10 9 8 7 6 5 4 3 2 1
Year   2004 2003 2002 2001 2000 1999

Copyright © 1999 Ian Dorton and Alex Smith

All rights reserved. This work is copyright. Permission is given for copies to be made of pages provided they are used exclusively within the institution for which this work has been purchased. For reproduction for any other purpose, permission must first be obtained in writing from the publishers.

Typeset by Wearset, Boldon, Tyne and Wear
Printed in Great Britain for Hodder & Stoughton Educational, a division of Hodder Headline Plc, 338 Euston Road, London NW1 3BH by Hobbs the Printers, Totton, Hants.

Table of Contents

Section 1	GENERAL DISCUSSION	
1	**Approaches to pre-issued case studies**	3
	A possible approach	3
	Case studies which arrive during holidays	5
	Sample marketing case study	5
2	**Approaches to terminal case study papers**	10
	Recommended approach	10
	Approach summary	13
3	**Approaches to project writing**	14
	A good knowledge of the requirements	14
	An organisation that will allow entry	14
	The choice of title	15
	Timing	15
	Structure	16
4	**Approaches to revision**	19
	Planning and organisation stage	19
	Familiarisation stage	21
	Learning stage	22
	Sitting the exam	22
Section 2	MODEL ANSWERS	
Unit 1	**The nature of business**	25
	The outrageous ambitions of Microsoft	25
Unit 2	**Organisational objectives**	29
	Levi – a comfortable fit	29
	The Fitness Plant sets strategic objectives	31
Unit 3	**The internal organisation of business**	35
	The restructuring of the Hunter Group	35
	Managing future success at Dixons	39
Unit 4	**Information and business decision making**	43
	Relaunching the Polo	43
	Promoting Aspen's communications equipment	47
Unit 5	**Financial accounting – Section A: Accounting and finance**	49
	The audit of Focus 2000	49
	Fortuna Education reconsider production in China	50
	The Redbrick Wine Distributors' balance sheet	52
	The sale of Land Cruiser Motors Ltd	53

Unit 5	**Financial accounting – Section B: Techniques used in the preparation of accounts**	**55**
	Body Care consider an attractive offer	55
	Sunshine Creek moves into a new market	58
	ChemClean takes in new stock	60
	Boddor undertakes a programme of cost cutting	62
Unit 5	**Financial accounting – Section C: Analysing accounts**	**65**
	Nelson forges ahead	65
	Harrison Components considers a major investment	68
	Noir Ltd grow with the skiing industry	70
Unit 6	**Management accounting – Section A: Budgeting**	**75**
	The Shoreham Nursery budget	75
	The JB Proctor budget	77
	A new stand for Waltham Town FC	78
	Warwick Ltd replace three vans	81
	Bedwyn Ltd choose a project	82
Unit 6	**Management accounting – Section B: Costing**	**85**
	Ninka Ltd's two cost centres	85
	Olympic Sports Shoe Ltd wishes to raise sales	87
	Financial data from the Mini Ohms Company	90
	A new speaker from Mobile Phone Accessories	91
Unit 7	**Human resource management**	**95**
	Blue Circle Cement changing its working practices	95
	Great Mills – Appointing and training new managers	98
Unit 8	**Operations management**	**103**
	Marks & Spencer decide on store location	103
	Allied Bakeries bread production	105
	ACD Video Ltd organise a major contract	108
	Baden and Clark develop a new production site	110
Unit 9	**Marketing**	**115**
	Quality Inns test the market	115
	Youth appeal – motoring: why Rover transformed the Metro	118
	Nike outsprints its rivals	120
	Sponsorship by Coca Cola	123
Unit 10	**The business environment – Section A: The market**	**127**
	The classical music business	127
	Coffee frost damage put at 40%	129
Unit 10	**The business environment – Section B: The macroeconomy**	**131**
	The China Company Ltd attempt to maintain margins	131
	Construction industry steeped in gloom	132
Unit 10	**The business environment – Section C: International business**	**135**
	Casper and Sons in Europe	135
	Clockwise Ltd deal with exchange rates	137
	Global competition	138

Unit 10	**The business environment – Section D: The influence of government**	**140**
	Difficult trading conditions for HEA Ltd	140
	The government budget affects Healstrome Ltd	142
Unit 10	**The business environment – Section E: The impact of the law**	**143**
	Playright Toys makes redundancies	143
	Pizza Village burns an employee	144
Unit 11	**Employer–employee relations**	**147**
	Yarrow workers vote for action over 2% pay offer	147
	A shock for Jaguar	149
	Low morale in hospital	152

ACKNOWLEDGEMENT

The author would like to thank the following: Beryl, Kim, John, Katie and Ellie.

SECTION

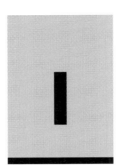

General Discussion

Approaches to pre-issued case studies

In a number of examination boards now, but especially for the Cambridge Modular, case studies are pre-issued, without the questions (!), for preparation to be undertaken by both teachers and students. It would be useful at this stage to consider possible approaches to the analysis of these case studies. To make it more simple, we can consider the approach for teachers, followed by advice for students.

Some teachers are fortunate enough to be in a large department, but others have to work on their own. Obviously, if a teacher is on their own, then the workload will be greater, but the overall approach should be the same.

The case studies are usually received four weeks before the actual examination date. If they are not received at the centre at the correct time, then they can be downloaded from the internet on the UCLES website, which is http://www.ucles.org.uk.

A POSSIBLE APPROACH

Most successful centres split their plans into four weekly blocks. A common approach is as follows:

Week 1   Teachers' activity

On receipt of the case study, there should be a meeting during which the responsibilities are shared out. In a perfect world, three documents should be produced as quickly as possible:

1 The first should be what is known as a **Background Report**, and it should include the basic information about the case study firm and those involved in it. It is meant to provide the background upon which students can base their answers. It is not meant to identify possible topics and issues. The usual items to be considered are:

a The type, and size, of firm involved. Is it a plc, or a Ltd company, or something else? The type and size of firm will have a great number of implications. It will affect the availability of funds, the legal position of the firm, the availability of economies of scale, and many other factors. So often, candidates suggest that small firms, with a turnover of only about £200,000 should use advertising on the television as their main form of promotion!

b The location of the firm. It is rarely a coincidence that the firms in case studies are located where they are. The paper setters often locate firms, and their suppliers and markets, in specific areas so that they can then ask questions requiring answers that can be improved by considering the actual location of firms, suppliers, and markets.

c The core activity of the firm. Is it involved in primary, secondary or tertiary activity? If it produces a tangible product, what production system is being used?

d The key characters in the case study. What are their names and what positions do they hold? Who is responsible to whom? An organisation chart is often useful here.

e SWOT analysis. This is always a useful activity in a background document.

This document should not be too long, but teachers will find that there are overlaps on many papers and that as they prepare their Background Reports, with suitable cutting and pasting on the word processor, the time taken to prepare the document gets less and the length of the document increases.

2 The second document is the **Issues Sheet**. This is obviously of great importance and it is in this document that the teacher needs to identify areas of the syllabus that have been flagged up in the case study. In larger departments, individuals can be asked to concentrate

upon specific areas of the syllabus. For example, in the Cambridge Modular Business Organisation case study, the Double Module, individual teachers might concentrate upon accounting and finance, human resources, operations management, and marketing. The important thing here is to make sure that you attempt to identify topic areas that are obviously important to the case, as opposed to attempting to spot exact questions that might arise. Thus, it would be sensible to identify that motivation is an obvious issue in a case study and then to cover all aspects of motivation, rather than to assume that the question would simply be 'How might motivation be improved at XYZ Ltd?'. The danger with the latter approach is that if the question asked relates to morale and factors identifying low morale, then the candidate may well give the prepared answer rather than concentrate upon the actual question posed. (A sample marketing case study, Background Report, and Issues Sheet, are given on pages 5, 6 and 9.)

3 The third document is the **Syllabus Sheet**. This is simply a copy of the relevant syllabus, or a copy of the teaching syllabus employed by the department. This is very important because the candidates must be aware that there is always likely to be at least one question on any given pre-issued case study that has not been flagged up by the case. Because of this, the candidate will require a working knowledge of the whole syllabus being tested.

Week 1   Students' activity

Students should have been issued with the case study and asked to prepare their own Background Reports and Issues Sheets. The importance of the Background Report should be stressed. In some centres, it is the responsibility of the students alone to prepare the Background Report.

Week 2   Teachers' activity

It is at this stage that the Background Report and Issues Sheet should be distributed to the students and then discussed in the light of the students' own comments and prepared documents. This process is extremely important, because it immediately gets the students involved in the case study and it also makes them feel that they are contributing. Indeed, it is rare for students not to spot something that the teachers have missed.

Week 2   Students' activity

Work in lessons should involve discussion on the Background Reports and Issues Sheets. It is essential that the students have a good understanding of the firm in question and that they have identified the key issues in the case. However, in their own time, they should be pursuing general revision of the syllabus, based upon the Syllabus Sheet.

Week 3   Teachers' activity

Teachers should continue to ensure that the students have a good grasp of the theory behind the issues that appear to be central to the case study. In addition, they should be setting up a procedure whereby the students can identify areas of difficulty in their general revision and then gain help to overcome the problems. This might involve voluntary revision clinics outside the timetable. Timed questions in class are often beneficial at this point.

Week 3   Students' activity

Students should be continuing to work on the case study topics in lessons and to undertake general revision in their own time. It is essential that they identify their own areas of weakness and that they make these known to their teachers.

Week 4   Teachers' activity

There should be at least one session on examination technique, centring upon the demands of a 'Levels of Response' approach to marking and also time management in the examination room. Otherwise, this is the time for final coverage of any outstanding areas of the syllabus. More timed questions might well be worthwhile.

Week 4   Students' activity

Students must ensure that they are aware of the format of the paper, the demands of the questions and the importance of using case study material in their answers. They should also go through their final revision of the syllabus content, ensuring that there are no gaps. The Syllabus Sheet can be used for this.

CASE STUDIES WHICH ARRIVE DURING HOLIDAYS

The problem created when case studies are received in the holidays or when students are on study leave can entail real headaches for teachers. There is no one ideal solution. In many cases, centres attempt to get around the problem by organising in-depth sessions for the students, where the students come in once a week for about three hours at a time. This is far from ideal, but it is probably the best way forward. The approach used above can still be followed, week by week, but careful planning of the sessions becomes of paramount importance. It is essential to have variety in such long teaching spells.

SAMPLE MARKETING CASE STUDY

Case study questions – The North Duxton Railway

1 With reference to a firm or firms of which you have direct knowledge, give a brief explanation of any **three** of the following:
   a market segmentation
   b market share
   c the product life cycle
   d personal selling
   e distribution channels. [3 × 5]
   Questions 2, 3 and 4 refer to the case study, but your answers should not necessarily be limited to the material in the case.

2 The pricing policy of the North Duxton Railway is based upon a 'cost-plus' approach. Evaluate critically any two other pricing methods that the railway might adopt. [15]

3 The sectional demand figures (in 000s) for the last three years are shown below. John Underwood wants to use them to forecast demand for the future.

	1996	1997	1998
Section 1	32	36	37
Section 2	92	90	94
Section 3	56	56	54

a Using time series analysis, calculate the trend figures for all possible sections. [3]
b Using the graph paper provided, forecast the demand for Section 2 in 1999. [4]
c Discuss the benefits and drawbacks that John may find by using time series analysis as a forecasting tool. [8]

4 John Underwood wishes to conduct extensive market research. Evaluate various methods of market research which might be used to gain the required information. [15]

Background information on The North Duxton Railway

The North Duxton Railway is a preserved steam railway, which was originally owned and run by railway enthusiasts. The line, which is 21 miles long and passes through an attractive area of the West Country, was closed down by the government in 1967. It joined two reasonably sized market towns. In 1974, Mark O'Dea, a self-confessed steam railway fanatic, organised a group of like minded people and bought the line and two station properties from British Rail. After a great deal of restoration work, mostly carried out by volunteers, the line was re-opened in 1977 as a tourist attraction.

After a slow start, the railway enjoyed a steady growth in demand which continued until the late 1980s. However, a combination of recession and increased competition from other attractions meant that demand very much slowed from then on. The figures for the last 12 years are shown in Table 1. The railway had been run as a private limited company but, in 1990, the railway became a public limited company. This was done in order to raise finance, so that much needed renovation and replacement of worn out rolling stock and equipment could take place. In addition, the stations at each end of the line were completely refurbished and, as well as the existing ticket offices and snack bars, a small shop, a bar and a children's play area were added to each.

Year	Passengers (000s)
1987	154
1988	160
1989	168
1990	177
1991	175
1992	168
1993	170
1994	173
1995	178
1996	180
1997	182
1998	185

Table 1 Total paying passengers – 1987 to 1998

In July 1998, John Underwood, a retired marketing manager from a highly successful furniture company, was persuaded to come out of retirement and to run the railway for a period of three years. He decided that he would spend six months gathering information and observing the running of the company and that he would then implement any changes that he felt were necessary.

The first thing that John did was to investigate the pricing policy and the different services on offer. The standard services and prices are shown in Table 2. In addition, John discovered that there were a number of special services:

1. 'Twilight Specials' are run in the High Season. These are evening trips, available for group booking, where the passengers are served with drinks before the return trip and are then given a meal on the journey. The price varies with the size of the group, but an average price would be around £25 per head. These have been very popular and the bar profits have been impressive on such occasions.

2. 'Thomas the Tank Engine' visits usually take place on Saturday mornings, again in the High Season. Children are given a journey on a train that is designed to look like Thomas the Tank Engine. They are also given a tour of one of the stations and a souvenir baseball cap.

3. 'Santa Specials', along the same lines as the 'Thomas the Tank Engine' visits, are run throughout the four weeks leading up to Christmas. On these occasions, children are given a small present by Santa Claus, rather than receiving the baseball cap.

4. 'School Educational Days' are offered in the Low Season. School parties are given the opportunity to undertake project work and to travel on the railway.

5. In addition to the above offers, there are a number of 'specials' that are specifically aimed

Service	High Season Price (Note 1)	Low Season Price (Note 1)
Single Fare – Adult (Note 2)	£3	£2.50
Return Fare – Adult	£5	£4
Single Fare – Child	£1.50	£1.25
Return Fare – Child	£2.50	£2
Family Fare – Adult (Note 3)	£4	£3
Family Fare – Child	£1	£1

Table 2 Standard services and prices for the North Duxton Railway as at 1st July 1998.

Note 1 The railway is closed in January and February, when all of the maintenance work is carried out. The High Season is June, July and August. The Low Season is from the beginning of March to the end of May and from the beginning of September to the end of December.

Note 2 An adult fare is charged to anyone of 16 years or over. Children under the age of 3 travel free.

Note 3 A family fare is a return journey. A family must consist of at least three people and there must be at least one adult and one child.

at steam railway enthusiasts. There are special weekends, when guest locomotives are borrowed from other railways and there are one and two day engine driving courses. Both of these take place in the Low Season.

After concluding his investigations and watching the railway run, John felt that he had identified a number of areas of concern:

1. Demand for the railway is highly seasonal. When John split the year into three sections, March to May, June to August, and September to December. He discovered that approximately 50% of annual passenger traffic was carried in the High Season and that there were often large queues and disappointed potential customers at this time.

2. A new theme park is due to open in the Spring of 2000, some 20 miles from the railway. Since the railway's competitors tend to be other tourist attractions, he is sure that this will take away some of their customers, but he does not know how many.

3. The company now employs 40 full-time staff and is a well established medium-sized firm, but the amateur-enthusiast approach still exists. There are no real targets or objectives for the workforce or management and job demarcation hardly exists. Many of the workers feel that they can handle almost any of the activities. This has led to a number of mistakes and accidents.

4. The company appears to have little understanding of the market and has conducted minimal market research. However, the one thing that is clear is that the market for the different services is highly segmented, with very different demand characteristics in each group. In spite of this, fares are set on a straight cost-plus basis and do not take any notice of the variations in demand. For instance, there is a potential demand for the early morning services from local people who simply wish to use the railway as a means of getting from one town to the other in order to go to work. However, although the marginal cost of these journeys is low, the standard fares charged are above those charged by local bus services and so most local people take the bus, even though it is slower.

5. There has been very little promotion undertaken. The main method employed is a colour brochure, including a timetable and price list, which is circulated to local hotels and tourist offices. Other than this, and the odd piece of publicity, the firm depends upon word of mouth communication.

Background Report for The North Duxton Railway

The legal set-up of the firm

The North Duxton Railway (NDR) was founded in 1974, and was re-opened in 1977. It was originally part of a state-owned enterprise, British Rail. It then became a private limited company, upon foundation in 1974, and was turned into a plc in 1990.

It is not a large firm, employing 40 full-time staff, and the access to economies of scale would not be great, because of the nature of the firm. There might be some purchasing economies for the shops and bars, but little else. We do not know the turnover of NDR, although 185,000 paying passengers, at an average fare of, say, £2.50, would give £462,500. However, this ignores all income from the special services and also income from the snack bars, bars and shops.

The location of the firm

NDR is situated in the West Country. This is a part of England that is very popular with tourists in the summer, so the seasonal demand is not surprising. It is also an area which, in parts, is notorious for traffic problems, especially in the summer. It is not the sort of area which people just happen across. People go there for a specific purpose, or live there. It is not like, for example, London, where people will visit for one thing, but then undertake a number of other activities. It tends to be rather remote from the larger cities, and thus the larger areas of population.

The core activity

NDR is supplying a service. It is a tertiary activity. There are a number of services on offer:

● Train journeys for locals, who just wish to go to work, or to the next town for some other purpose.
● Train journeys for tourists.
● Special services, which are aimed at different interest groups and market segments.
● Extra, peripheral, services, such as the shops, bars, and play areas.

Remember that because it is a service, people have to go to it. It cannot be delivered. Thus, marketing should be a key activity. People have to be persuaded to go there, which is much harder than selling a good.

The key characters

Mark O'Dea   One of the founder owners, when the Ltd company was set up. He is presumably the major shareholder, and there is no reason to assume that this did not continue when the firm became a plc. He is a 'self-confessed steam railway fanatic' and this might affect his views of how the firm should be run. How objective can he be?

John Underwood   Retired marketing manager. Now managing director of NDR for three years. Short time scale and not a young man. He has been investigating the running of the firm for six months.

The workforce   There are 40 full-time workers. The workers have little specialisation and there is an implication of inefficiency.

SWOT analysis

Remember that strengths and weaknesses tend to be internal and opportunities and threats tend to be external.

Strengths

1 The company is established and has a keen central following of steam train enthusiasts.

2 John Underwood is conducting an investigation into the running of the firm.

3 The numbers of customers has increased steadily year on year.

4 The rolling stock and equipment have been renovated and replaced and the stations have been refurbished.

5 The special services seem to be very successful.

Weaknesses
1 John Underwood is not a young man.
2 Demand is very seasonal.
3 There is a new theme park opening in the near future.
4 There have been mistakes and accidents, because the workforce seem to think that they can handle almost any of the activities.
5 Knowledge of the market, pricing, and promotion, seems to be minimal.

Opportunities
1 In general, the demand for leisure facilities is increasing, as people become more wealthy.
2 There is excess demand in the summer, which needs to be satisfied.
3 There is a potential demand for the early morning services.

Threats
1 A continuing recession.
2 The new theme park.

Issues Sheet for The North Duxton Railway

There are a number of possible issues that have been flagged up in the case:

Issue 1 Differing objectives
● There may be differences of opinions between Mark O'Dea, who might adopt an amateur approach to the firm, and John Underwood, who is a professional manager and not an enthusiast.

Issue 2 The seasonal demand
● Demand has been seen to be seasonal. How might this be counteracted?

Issue 3 Table 1
● Table 1 is a perfect chance to ask a question regarding time series analysis.

Issue 4 The new theme park
● '... he is sure that this will take away some of his customers, but he does not know how many.' Market research methods to discover this?

Issue 5 The workforce
● Target setting and objectives, demarcation, and lack of specialisation. Is this on the syllabus?

Issue 6 Market research
● Segmented markets. Who to ask? (Sampling); How to ask? (Surveys); What to ask? (Questionnaires).

Issue 7 Pricing
● Different pricing methods – cost-plus at the moment.
● Marginal cost and contribution.
● Price elasticity of demand.
● Table 2 Price discrimination.

Issue 8 Promotion
● How could the promotional strategy be improved?

Issue 9 Marketing strategy
● This is a possibility in every marketing paper and so must be considered.

As can be seen from the questions asked to the case study on page 00 the major issues have been raised by the Issues Sheet.

Pricing policy and market research were both raised, although a wide knowledge of the topics is required, especially for the pricing question.

Time series analysis was also spotted, although the examiner has added a rather nice twist, by giving different figures and requiring a 3-point moving average. However, if the topic of time series analysis has been revised properly, then the students should be able to deal with the question well.

2 Approaches to terminal case study papers

In many business studies examination papers, candidates are presented with an unseen case study and then asked to answer questions based upon their knowledge of the appropriate syllabus, and to apply their responses to the situation in the case study. There are a number of different approaches that can be taken to this sort of paper, but the one outlined below seems to have worked very well for those who have adopted it. It is best to split the process into steps.

■ RECOMMENDED APPROACH

Step 1   Equipment

The candidates should ensure that they enter the examination room with a highlighter pen and some form of time-piece. This is essential for carrying out the preparation of the paper and also for avoiding spending longer on any single question than the marks available merit. The uses of both instruments will become clear as we proceed.

Step 2   Read and highlight the case

When the instruction is given to start the examination, the candidate should read the case study paper, highlighting the important areas. It is important, at this stage, that the candidate does not read the questions that go with the case study. It has been shown that if candidates read the questions before they read the case study, it can affect the way that they read it. Once the candidate has it in his or her mind that the questions cover certain areas, the reading of the case study tends to become selective and it is easy for important parts of the text to be overlooked, because they are considered to be irrelevant to the questions. It is also important that the candidate does not highlight too much of the text, since it makes the process pointless. In general, any important names, the type of the firm, e.g. plc or Ltd, and any obvious areas of the syllabus that are being flagged up, should be marked.

An example is given below:

Insurance Telecommunication Services Ltd

Insurance Telecommunication Services Ltd (ITS) provides opportunity for direct contact between insurance companies and their customers via the telephone. In this way the insurance company is able to deal directly with customers, rather than selling its products through the more traditional channel intermediaries of agents or brokers. By direct selling the insurance company no longer has to pay the intermediary's commission and consequently is able to price its products more keenly. In a very competitive market, where price is regarded as a major influence on the consumer's purchase decision, being able to quote a lower insurance premium offers an insurance company a significant competitive advantage. An additional benefit of direct selling is that the insurance company is able to gather valuable market knowledge about its customers. As the insurance industry is underpinned by the concept of pooled risk any company capable of screening out high-risk business is better placed to make profits.

As we can see on page 10, the candidate will have identified the name of the business and the legal structure, i.e. it is a private limited company. Possible issues identified are communication, channels of distribution, pricing and price elasticity of demand, competition, and market research.

Step 3 Read and highlight the questions

Only when the case study has been read through and highlighted should the candidate take the next step, which is to look at the questions. The candidate should go through the question identifying and highlighting the 'Question Prompt' and the area of the syllabus being tested. For example:

- Using SWOT analysis, evaluate the market situation facing XYZ Ltd at the present time.

The area of the syllabus is obviously SWOT analysis and the candidate is expected to take an evaluative approach to the question. The 'Question Prompt' is the key word used in the question that tells the candidate exactly what level of response the examiner is expecting. There are a limited number of these prompts and candidates should be aware of them. Common prompts and their meanings are shown on page 12.

Step 4 Identify the marks and time available for each question

Once the candidate has highlighted the questions, the next matter to consider is the marks for each question and the time available. As has already been said, the marks available for each question will give a good indication of the depth of response required by the examiner. However, the marks can also be used to allocate time to each response. For example, if we imagine a three hour examination worth a total of 100 marks, then the allocation of time per mark can be worked out as follows:

Total time available	180 minutes
Preparation time	15 minutes
Remaining time	165 minutes
Time per mark	1½ minutes
Spare time at end	15 minutes

This is easy for the candidate, who simply has to take the marks available for a question and then add half again in order to know how much time should be spent on it. Thus, a 20 mark question should be worked on for 30 minutes and a 5 mark question for 7½ minutes. This approach avoids one of the great examination dangers, which is spending too long on a question that does not have enough marks to merit the attention. However, it takes great fortitude for candidates to break off from a question when the time is up and the importance of doing so must be continually stressed by teachers.

Step 5 Re-read in the light of the questions

Once the question prompts, syllabus areas, and timings for the questions, have been identified, the candidate should read through the case study again, identifying any areas that were missed the first time, especially in the light of the questions that are to be answered. Whilst more highlighting may now be necessary, it should be remembered that only essential matters should be identified.

Step 6 Answering the questions

Now the questions should be attempted, and it is usually best to approach them in the order in which they have been written. Although they are not supposed to, examiners often write questions that follow a certain order in the case and, if this occurs, it is often easier to do a later question when an earlier one has already been completed. It is often said that candidates should start with their best answer, but in the case of unseen case study papers, this would not really be advisable.

Question Type and Question Prompt examples	Meaning and comments
CALCULATION E.g. calculate … What percentage … Describe the trend … Comment on the trend …	This is usually straightforward and expects a numerical outcome. However, candidates should always show their working, because they will get reward for anything that is correct, even if their final answer is wrong. If asked to write about trends, the candidates should remember that this does not mean describing every movement of the data, e.g. 'it went up in 1995, down in 1996, down again in 1997, etc'. The trend is the general direction that data takes, i.e. it rises, falls, or stays the same. If possible, candidates should always state any assumptions that they have made in their calculations.
EXPLAIN Explain the meaning of … Explain, giving reasons … Explain why … Explain how and why …	This is usually a prompt looking for lower order responses. A simple explanation of the syllabus area being tested, in the context of the case study, will usually suffice to score a good mark on the question.
DISCUSS Discuss the alternatives … Discuss the methods … Discuss the factors … Discuss the advantages and disadvantages …	This almost always is intended to make the candidates be evaluative in their answers. The answers are supposed to identify the key elements in the question and then evaluate them. There are two simple methods for candidates to use in order to evaluate. One is to list the elements and then to identify the most important, obviously explaining the reason for the choice. The second is to adopt a short run/long run policy, identifying factors that will change or will apply in different time scales.
WHAT What would be the main factors … What methods …	This is a difficult prompt and the expectations vary. Usually, it means evaluate, but it is not always easy to decide. If unsure, the candidate should look at the number of marks available for the question. This is usually a good indicator of the depth of response expected by the examiner.
EVALUATE Evaluate the role … Evaluate the implications … Evaluate different methods …	This is obviously a very simple prompt and the candidate needs to adopt the same approach as that described for 'Discuss' above.
OUTLINE A STRATEGY Devise a marketing strategy for … What promotional strategy …	This is becoming a very popular prompt and tests many skills. Candidates must ensure that they offer a strategy and not simply an unconnected list of suggestions. A strategy is a combination of factors and an awareness that the factors should be connected. Too often, candidates make individual suggestions that clash with each other. For example, they suggest that a firm should increase promotion, improve the product, increase distribution, and lower the price of the product. Thus, they are rapidly increasing costs whilst, possibly, reducing revenue. It would be much more simple to say that they might improve the product and use the improvement to attempt to gain consumer loyalty which will lead to inelastic demand, enabling the firm to raise price and thus revenue.

Table 3 Common prompts and their meanings

APPROACH SUMMARY

The whole approach can be expressed in a number of bullet points:

- Be prepared for the examination, with highlighter and time-piece.
- Read through the case study, before looking at the questions.
- Highlight the important points.
- Read through the questions.
- Highlight the question prompts and syllabus areas being tested.
- Identify the marks available for each question.
- Use these marks to evaluate the importance of each question.
- Use these marks to identify the time to be spent on each question.
- Re-read the case study in the light of the questions.
- Start to answer the questions, in order.
- Ensure that the time limits for each question are observed.
- Use any time left at the end to check your work.

3 Approaches to project writing

A great many courses in Business Studies now include the need to write a piece of coursework, or a project. In most cases, the piece of work takes the form of a research question based upon a real business. Students should view projects in a good light, since it is the one time in the examination process that the student is in charge. It is a chance for the student to take control and to develop expertise in an area of the student's choice. As long as the student works within the criteria laid down by the examination board, then the student is free to do whatever he or she wishes.

There are a number of points that need to be considered, if a good project is to be generated:

A GOOD KNOWLEDGE OF THE REQUIREMENTS

It is essential that the teacher and student become aware of the formal demands of the examination board in question. This will change from board to board, but on the whole, there is little actual difference in expectations and required standards. From the Cambridge Board to the International Baccalaureate, the main requirement is for a project that takes a problem solving approach, preferably to a real life problem, showing clear definition, objectives, analysis, evaluation and conclusions. If possible, the teacher and student should get a copy of the assessment criteria and then devise a framework for the project that will enable the assessment criteria to be met. An example of assessment criteria (this one is from the UCLES Modular Business Studies Research Assignment) is shown below:

No.	Criteria	Marks possible
1	The skill with which the problem has been put into context and considered.	10
2	Evidence of personal research.	15
3	Evidence of understanding of relevant business studies concepts and ideas.	15
4	Application of business studies concepts and ideas to the problem.	15
5	The logic and breadth of the analysis undertaken.	15
6	Evaluation of alternatives and conclusion related to problem set.	20
7	Quality of language.	5
8	Other aspects of presentation, including appropriate use of tables, graphs and charts, etc.	5
		100

Table 4 An example of assessment criteria

In most cases, examiners will work to a much more detailed set of assessment criteria than the one published by the board and, if possible, the teacher should try to get hold of a copy of one of those. If the board in question will not supply it, telephone networking around schools and colleges in the area will normally unearth an examiner who will photocopy the sheet for the teacher!

AN ORGANISATION THAT WILL ALLOW ENTRY

The choice of an organisation in which to carry out the research is critical to the success of the project. The organisation can be a private firm, a government or local government department, a charity, or even a school. The key thing is that, whatever the organisation, they will allow the student to have access to the information and figures that are required. Too often, students go into organisations and are then told, too late, that they can have no access to financial figures or, almost as bad, that they can only use figures from three or four years ago. One way around this is for students to, in effect, set up their own firms. Thus, they might look at the feasibility of setting up a new clothes shop in the local high street. If the worst comes to the worst, this can be quite a reasonable option.

The choice of organisation can be made in a number of ways. Sometimes it comes through family links, or the relatives of friends. Other sources might be part-time jobs, past work experience placements, or organisations that the student belongs to, such as a gym or sports team. Another possibility is to conduct research in the vicinity of an organisation, without needing the precise help of that organisation. An example of this sort of project might be a queuing simulation at the local station or at a local car park. The success of this sort of project will obviously depend upon the quality of the primary research undertaken.

THE CHOICE OF THE TITLE

Along with the choice of organisation, this is the other critical activity in the writing of a good project. It is essential that the title leads to a problem that has to be solved, or a decision that has to be made. Too often, projects tend to be descriptive and this is often a consequence of the title chosen. An example of this might be: 'An investigation into the profitability of XYZ Ltd over the past five years.' This sort of project is almost bound to be historic and descriptive.

In general, there are a few rules that should be stuck to when choosing a title:

● The title should be expressed in the form of a question, or should be backed up by a research question. Thus one might get: 'Should XYZ Ltd purchase or rent their car fleet?', or one might have a title of, 'Car fleet management at XYZ Ltd' and the previous title is then stated as the research question.
● The title should represent a relatively small problem and not one that is obviously beyond the scope of a student writing within the stated assessment criteria. Thus, one should avoid titles like: 'How can Lloyds Bank plc improve its profitability?' and go for titles such as: 'Is it possible to significantly reduce costs in the post-room at the Lloyds Bank regional office in xxx, whilst retaining the quality of service?'.
● The title should relate to a problem that is current or a decision that has yet to be made. When candidates try to explain problems that have already happened, or decisions that have already been made, they invariably fall into the trap of becoming descriptive.

A good, precisely stated title, posed as a question and relating to a relatively small problem or decision is the aim. However, the candidate should remember that the title will often change a little as the project is worked on and the information is collected. In many cases, candidates have started projects on such things as improving profits, found out that they are allowed cost information, but not information on revenue, and have still written good projects simply based on cost reduction.

TIMING

Candidates usually have a relatively large amount of time in which to investigate and write up their projects. This is necessary, but can often be the downfall of the less organised candidate. There is a tendency to think that there is so much time available that commencement of the research can always be put off. This belief is fatal. Teachers should stress again and again to students that they must begin work as soon as possible and that they will be checked for progress at specific points in the writing period.

Although it is hard to generalise, it should take at least four weeks for a student to write up a reasonable project, after the research has been done. This allows for all the other commitments that the student might have. Thus students must be aware that they should have finished their research phase of the project at least four weeks before the set submission date.

It can also be beneficial if the project is finished before the date set, since there will then be time for review and possible last minute alterations. The project that is finished at the very last minute will almost invariably have faults that could have been spotted and rectified, if more time had been available.

▮ STRUCTURE

If a project is well structured, then the battle is almost won. If the problem is clearly defined, in context, and a clear set of objectives is stated, then the project should almost write itself. After many years of experimentation, the authors have finally arrived at the following blueprint of what a successful project should contain:

1. **Title Page** This may appear an obvious requirement, but too often there is no title page on a project or it is not clear what the title is. The page should state the title, the candidate name, and also the candidate's number. It is also helpful to include the name of the school or college.

2. **Abstract** The examiner can be helped by a short abstract page, describing the setting, aims, analysis, conclusions and recommendations of the project. This sheet is normally written last and is not a specific requirement. However, anything that helps the examiner might be beneficial in the long run!

3. **Index** This should be clear and show the main chapter headings and the pages upon which they should be found. Project pages should always be numbered. This is obviously one of the last pages to be prepared, but it is an important part of the presentation of the work.

4. **Terms of Reference** A simple statement of who the research is for, what it is about, where the student comes from, and when the project was due. It is often signed. A typical Terms of Reference Statement might be:

> This research assignment has been requested by ... (*either the name/s of the members of staff involved or the names of the owners/managers of the organisation involved*). It is an investigation into ... (*e.g. how labour turnover at XYZ Ltd might be reduced*).
>
> I am a Grade 12 student at United World College studying Business and Organisation Higher Level for the International Baccalaureate Diploma.
>
> The submission date for the project is ... (*day/month/year*).
>
> Name ...

5. **Context and the Problem** This is usually headed as 'Introduction'. It can be split into two sections, 'Introduction to the Organisation' and 'Introduction to the Problem or Decision'. The introduction to the organisation should make clear the legal set up of the firm, as well as its precise location and size. The relevant operations of the firm should also be outlined. The introduction to the problem or decision should always start with a re-statement of the research question. The problem or decision to be made should then be explained in the context of the organisation in question.

6. **Objectives** This is possibly the most important section of the project because, if done well, it will act as a plan for the rest of the investigation. The objectives can be split into three headings, general objectives, specific objectives, and the objectives of the organisation. The general objective is a re-wording of the title and then the specific objectives are the steps that need to be taken in order to achieve the general objective. The organisation's objectives are a statement of what the firm hopes to come from the investigation. Objectives should state intentions and outcomes, and not just intentions.

It is possibly best to illustrate this by using the following example. Let us consider the title:

Should XYZ Ltd continue to buy their company cars or should they lease them?

The General Objective might be: 'To decide whether XYZ Ltd should continue to buy their company cars or lease them?'

The Specific Objectives might be:

a To investigate the present situation at XYZ Ltd in order to be able to understand the decision and to be able to put it into context.
b To discover the views of those affected by the decision in order to gain a wide view.
c To ascertain the costs of running the present system of company car purchase in order to make a comparison.
d To ascertain the costs of leasing the company cars in order to make a comparison.
e To compare the costs of purchase and leasing in order to move towards a decision.
f To consider any non-monetary factors that might need to be taken into account in order to reach a decision.
g To come to a conclusion and to make recommendations.
h To evaluate the running of the investigation in order to assess possible weaknesses in the decision making.

These objectives should enable the student to plan the rest of the project. Objective 1 helps to write the introduction and then the other objectives each become sections or chapter headings. Thus, if the Introduction is Section 1, then Section 2 is Objectives, Section 3 is Procedures, and the rest of the sections are based upon the specific objectives from 2 to 8. Section 4 could be headed: 'The views of those affected by the decision.' Section 5 could be: 'The costs of running the present system of car purchase.' And so on.

The organisation's objectives might be:

- To identify the least cost method of car purchase.
- To maintain morale and motivation amongst the employees.

The student would have to bear in mind the possible conflict in these objectives when conducting the research.

---

7 **Procedures** This is the last section before the project research and analysis gets underway. It identifies the business studies concepts and techniques that will need to be employed in order to achieve the specific objectives of the project and thus to come to a sensible conclusion. Procedures are normally a set of statements of intent. It is easiest to show this by example. The procedures relating to the first two specific objectives used in the example above might be:

a Procedure 1 In order to achieve Objective 1, I need to use desk research to gain secondary information on the background of the firm. I will also need to use primary research to gain an overview of the current purchasing system and the problems with it.

b Procedure 2 In order to achieve Objective 2, I need to use primary research in the form of interviews and questionnaires. This will generate important primary information.

8 **The main information and analysis sections** These have already been explained. They are based upon the specific objectives and cover all of the data collection, presentation, and analysis necessary for a successful outcome to the investigation.

9 **Conclusions** This section should tie together the analysis that has been made and should clearly state the major findings. The conclusions should obviously relate to the objectives. Indeed, there is nothing wrong with

going through each of the objectives in turn and stating the conclusions relating to the attainment of the objectives.

10 **Recommendations**   Here, the options available should be stated and then a reasoned answer, supported by the research, should be submitted.

11 **Evaluation**   As already stated, this final section should be an attempt by the student to identify areas of strength and weakness in the project. Admission of weakness will not lower the student in the eyes of the examiner. Indeed, it might do quite the reverse. The ability to recognise weaknesses is an evaluative skill and may well be rewarded.

12 **Appendices**   Any support matter that is not essential to the main body of the project, but that would help to give background, should be included here. There should always be a bibliography and, if appropriate, a glossary of technical terms used.

Project writing can be a hugely rewarding activity, for both students and teachers. If a sensible, well structured and well timed, approach is taken, then success is within the reach of all, not just the most gifted. Much of project writing relates to determination and interest.

4 Approaches to revision

Revision for Business Studies is little different to revision in any other subject and it is to be hoped that this section will help students to revise in all of their areas of study. Revision can best be broken down into four stages:

- Planning and organisation
- Familiarisation
- Learning
- Sitting the exam.

As usual, we shall deal with each of these in turn.

PLANNING AND ORGANISATION STAGE

If we assume that the student is going to be sitting terminal examinations in June, then the planning and organisation stage of revision should begin about three months before the examinations are due to start. The planning and organisation phase can be broken down into a number of discrete areas:

Objective setting

Like any good Business Studies student, the first thing that the candidate should do is to set objectives and, as always, these objectives should be primary and secondary. The primary objective is usually straight forward. It is to achieve the best possible grades in the examinations. The secondary objectives are those that need to be achieved if the primary objective is to be reached. These objectives need to be specific, challenging and achievable. They also need to be measurable. For example: 'To work as hard as I can' is not a good objective, but 'To read all my notes on Critical Path Analysis and to go through four questions on it' is. For the second, it is easy to see if the objective has been achieved.

Objectives should be set for all areas of the planning and organisation phase. They are an over-arching part of the preparation for effective revision.

Timing

It is essential that the student plans his or her time effectively for the weeks running up to the examinations. The time planning should be related to both study and leisure time. There is no point in just organising study time. Leisure is essential, if a student is going to be relaxed enough to study effectively. It is not possible to work all the time, and so it is advisable to plan the time to be taken off. Continued lesson time at school or college, before study leave, also needs to be taken into account, as do planned holidays or breaks. On the subject of breaks or holidays, there is nothing wrong with having breaks from revision, so long as they are planned and thus accounted for in the overall scheme.

A weekly chart, such as the example given in Table 5, may prove to be of use. It is essential that the student writes down a study plan, and then ticks off the sessions as they are achieved. If this does not happen, then it is easy to miss sessions and to fool oneself that all will be well. The human memory can be very selective! If the evidence of non-achievement is written down, then it is a great deal harder to ignore.

Some students prefer to spend a whole day on one subject and others like to mix it up. There are advantages and disadvantages to both approaches and it should really come down to the personal preference of the individual.

Before study leave, the student will only have to plan time in the evenings and at weekends. The plan in Table 5 is, obviously, the sort of week that could be planned during study leave.

As we can see, the student does not attempt to work all the time, it would be counter-productive to do so. No session lasts

Week: 7							
	Monday	Tuesday	Wed.	Thursday	Friday	Saturday	Sunday
09.00 to 10.30	Business Studies – CPA	History – Pitt & Fox	English – *Wuthering Heights*	Business Studies – Pricing	History – The Liberals	English – *Othello*	No study
11.00 to 12.30	Business Studies – Simulation	History – Italian unification	English – *The Tempest*	Business Studies – Promotion	History – Russia 1905–1917	English – *The Tempest*	No study
14.00 to 15.30	English – *Othello*	Business Studies – Market research	History – Gladstone and Disraeli	English – Unseen prac. crit.	Business Studies – Marketing strategy	No study	History – Tories 1815–1830
16.00 to 17.30	English – Chaucer	Business Studies – Production	History – German unification	English – Chaucer	Business Studies – Break-even	No study	History – The Whig reforms
Early evening	General reading, if able	General reading, if able	General reading, if able	General reading, if able	General reading, if able	No study	General reading, if able
After 20.00	No study	No study	No study	No study	No study	No study	No study

Table 5 Sample revision sheet for a student sitting 'A' Levels in Business Studies, English and History

more than one and a half hours, and the student works a maximum of six hours in the normal day. The early evening session is an optional one, in which the student can choose to work or not, and in which the subject to be studied is up to the student.

Physical care

It is essential that the student attempts to stay fit and well in the run up to the examinations. Whilst illness does sometimes occur, through no fault of the student, the likelihood can be minimised by taking certain steps. The main elements to an effective physical care programme are a balanced diet, moderate, but regular, physical exercise, and sensible sleeping habits.

The key element of these may well be sleeping habits. If a revision plan is to work, then it is essential that the student gets up each morning in time to start the first work period punctually. This is unlikely to happen if the student was out late the night before, and so a sensible time to go to bed is essential in the normal week. The plan offered above takes this into account and allows for a late night on Saturdays by having no planned work on the Sunday morning.

Planning of the working environment

The student should ensure that the area in which he or she is going to work is conducive to study. However, the best conditions for study will vary from student to student. As a general rule, it is thought that most people study best if they work in silence, under medium lighting, sitting up at a desk or table. However, some people dislike silence and work better with music playing, and others do not like the formality of sitting at a desk. It is up to the individual student to identify their personal requirements for an effective working environment and to ensure that this is provided. Whatever the choice, it should be remembered that the examination will take place in the traditional setting of a formal examination hall, with complete silence.

Organisation of revision scripts

This is probably the most important process in the planning and organisation stage and it takes the most amount of time. It is essential that the student prepares a revision script for each of the subjects to be taken. The starting point is the syllabus for the subject. It is from the syllabus that the examiner sets the paper and so it is to the syllabus that the student must go in order to plan and produce a revision script.

The syllabus should be looked at and then broken down into major topic areas. Thus, for Business Studies, this might be Human Resource Management, Financial and Managerial Accounting, Marketing, Operations Management, and Economics.

Once the major topic areas have been identified, then they should be broken down in turn, to give the main topics within each area. Once this has been done, the student needs to go through all of his or her notes, essays, worked examples, and hand-outs, and organise them under the topic headings. It is at this stage that the student may realise that there are certain areas where there is a lack of useful revision material and that additional notes may be needed.

Once all has been organised, then the student can begin to write revision notes, based upon the information collected. These notes should ideally take a layered format. Whether they are on index cards or file paper, the same applies. The first sheet should have the general topic, the next sheet should have the main areas under the topic, the sheet after should have the main areas with more detail, and so on. In other words, the degree of detail should increase as one moves down the pile of index cards or through the stack of file paper.

This is a time consuming process, but it has a number of plus points. The student often gains confidence from having created the revision scripts and the sheer act of creation begins the revision process and the accumulation of knowledge.

FAMILIARISATION STAGE

If the planning and organisation stage has been started about three months before the examinations, then the familiarisation stage can begin immediately the revision scripts have been prepared. The preparation time for the revision scripts might be as much as six weeks, so the familiarisation might begin about six weeks before the examinations are due to start.

The familiarisation stage is about understanding and not learning. The learning part comes later. It is in the familiarisation stage that the work routine is especially established, particularly when the period of study leave has begun.

In these periods, emphasis should be placed upon two things:

1 Understanding the concepts in the revision scripts and ensuring that there are no areas of confusion or doubt.

2 Practising answers to questions of the type that will be encountered in the actual examinations. A mixture of timed and non-timed responses should be employed. In addition, the student should ensure that they are aware of the exact demands that will be made in the various examination papers. The length of each paper, the number of questions to be answered, the choice involved (if any), and the specific requirements should be familiarised. Too many students have come a cropper by answering two questions from the same section of a paper, when only one was allowed!

Another important activity in the familiarisation stage is for the candidate, with the aid of the teacher, to begin to prioritise areas of revision. From past experience and by the analysis of past papers, it is possible to highlight areas of the syllabus that are regularly tested and areas that are relatively ignored. Once this has been done, then the percentage of time given to those areas should be adjusted accordingly, with much less being given over to the unpopular topics. Whilst not attempting to question spot, it still makes sense to be aware of the particular leanings of examiners and paper setters.

LEARNING

In the two or three weeks immediately before the examinations, it is time for the candidate to stop using the revision scripts as a prompt and to begin to memorise the important areas and lists of key facts that will be necessary for a good performance. It is at this stage where it might be advisable to reduce the length of revision periods to one hour and the time spent on revision in the whole day to about five hours. This is necessary because the revision periods are now more demanding and thus more tiring.

At this stage, it would be sensible to concentrate on the key areas of the syllabus that were highlighted in the familiarisation stage.

SITTING THE EXAM

We have already considered the matter of actually sitting the examinations in the section on Approaches to Terminal Case Study Papers (pages 10 to 13). Students should take note of the advice offered on equipment, reading and highlighting questions, and identifying the marks and time available for each question. They should also look at the final part (page 11) on answering the question.

In conclusion

Revision, like almost anything else, is a series of skills and, if students prepare properly and gain the correct skills, then examinations should hold few fears and success will be highly likely – good luck.

SECTION 2

Model Answers

UNIT 1

The nature of business

THE OUTRAGEOUS AMBITIONS OF MICROSOFT

Student book pages 10–12

1 Microsoft is a multinational organisation. This means that it has its headquarters in the United States, but it carries out its operations, such as the publishing of computer software, in a number of different countries. It is a public company in the USA, issuing shares on the US stock market.

2 **a** The size of Microsoft has been measured by the size of its sales revenue which is $4.65 billion.
b Computer software publishing involves the design of the software and then its production. The software design itself is a labour intensive process but employs relatively few workers relative to the sales of Microsoft. The production of the software will be a capital intensive process and again will employ relatively few workers relative to the size of Microsoft. Thus Microsoft would look a much smaller company if it was measured by the number of people it employs compared to measuring it by turnover. The key thing here is that any comparison of size with other firms in the software publishing industry should be done on the same basis. For example, comparing Microsoft and Apple Mackintosh should be done on revenue.

3 Microsoft has grown quickly since its foundation in 1975 for the following reasons:

● **The growth in the market.** The demand for PCs and software is positively related to people's incomes; as incomes have increased this has increased the demand for IT products. As technology in the IT industry has developed the industry has grown. As more and more organisations and people own PCs there is an increase in demand for their applications. Word processing and spreadsheets are now possible on ordinary PCs. The software produced by Microsoft fulfils this demand.

● **Microsoft's success within the market.** Microsoft has been successful within the IT market and has managed to gain an increasing share of this growing market. Microsoft has been successful at producing products such as Windows, a product that has out-competed its rivals in the market.

● **Bill Gates' management of the organisation.** As a leader of the company Bill Gates has pushed to continuously expand Microsoft. For example, his plans to create Microsoft Network, a global on-line service supplying information.

4 **a** As Microsoft has increased in size it will have benefited from internal economies of scale. These economies mean that the firm's unit costs of production will fall as its scale of production increases. Microsoft could have benefited from the following:

● **Commercial economies**, where Microsoft can buy and sell in bulk. The components it needs to produce its software can be bought in larger quantities which means that supplies will offer Microsoft lower prices per unit. As Microsoft sells larger quantities of its software programmes it will be able to reduce the unit costs of selling as the costs of selling are spread across a larger number of units. For example, the $25,000 salary paid to the salesperson who sells 20,000 units per year gives a unit cost per worker of ($25,000/20,000) = $1.20 of sales, whereas the $50,000 paid to a salesperson in a larger organisation who sells 100,000 units per year is ($50,000/100,000) = $0.50.

- **Financial economies.** Microsoft will have the advantage of being able to raise funds at a lower cost per unit as a large organisation because it represents a lower risk to lenders. By raising funds in large quantities the cost per $ falls as administrative costs are spread over a larger quantity of output.
- **Managerial economies.** Managers at Microsoft will be able to specialise in their specific functions which increases their efficiency.
- **Technical economies.** Larger production runs and more technically advanced capital available to Microsoft will improve its efficiency as it increases in size. As more advanced computer software design equipment becomes available Microsoft as a large organisation can take advantage of it.

Microsoft will also have benefited from external economies of scale as the entire IT industry expands. It will have been able to hire staff that have been trained by other organisations and learn from the technological breakthroughs made by competing companies.

b When the scale of Microsoft's operation expands it will experience diseconomies of scale that will reduce its efficiency as an organisation:

- **Information diseconomies.** The complex hierarchies that often exist in large firms will reduce the effectiveness of the flows of information between people within the organisation and, as a result, reduce their effectiveness. For example, senior managers at Microsoft might want to gain information from their sales force; because this has to pass through a number of layers in a hierarchy it will reduce the quality of the information coming through. However, it is possible that a large firm with more funds can generate better quality information from its systems. For example, an administration department can be employed to manage the flow of information effectively.
- **Human diseconomies.** Once Microsoft reaches a certain size, the workforce may lose its sense of association with such a large organisation and may not work with the same amount of motivation as they had done in such a small compact unit. It is possible, however, that a large company like Microsoft, with a specialist personnel department, can apply human relations techniques to improve the motivation of the workforce.

As an organisation like Microsoft increases in size it will certainly experience the diseconomies of scale identified above, it is the skill with which the organisation deals with these difficulties that determines how problematic they are.

5 As Microsoft grew its stakeholders would have benefited in the following ways:

- Microsoft's shareholders would have seen the value of the company they own rise. As more and more profit is made by the company it be retained by the business and added to the value of funds attributable to the shareholders. The profit can also be distributed by the company in the form of dividends and paid to Microsoft's shareholders.
- Microsoft's employees will have gained through the growth in the company in the form of increased employment opportunities as more jobs are created within the business. They may well have also enjoyed greater job security. As Microsoft's profitability rises with its growth it could mean

higher wages, bonuses and fringe benefits for the employees.
- As Microsoft grows it will produce a wider range of products and more sophisticated products. The profit generated can be put into research and development which produces new, better products, such as Windows 97.
- Suppliers of Microsoft will see an increase in demand for their products as Microsoft needs to produce more of its own products and needs more inputs.
- Financiers, such as banks, will be pleased with the greater security of their funds as more funds flow into Microsoft. With growth also comes an increase in demand for finance which will give the banks greater profitability.
- As Microsoft grows it will lead to greater employment opportunities within the local community. It will also generate more income for the local economy as people are employed by Microsoft and suppliers of Microsoft are attracted to the local area.

6 As a multinational company Microsoft will receive the following benefits:

- It will be operating in close proximity to the local market and will be able to make better informed decisions about operating in that local market. For example, the needs of software supplied to the French market can be best designed by listening to French consumers. Judgements can also be made about the best way to distribute the product in the local market. Where do French consumers expect to buy their software products?
- By operating in different countries Microsoft can gain cost advantages. In India, for example, there is a plentiful supply of cheap, highly skilled workers who can produce Microsoft products at low costs.
- By operating as a multinational, Microsoft will be able to avoid the trade barriers that apply to normal exports it makes from the USA into countries that operate trade barriers.
- Microsoft will benefit from lower transport costs that arise from overseas production compared to shipping domestically produced products abroad. If the goods were produced in the target market by another company under licence, then Microsoft would not be able to guarantee the quality of the products produced under its name.
- Any company that expands its business overseas will benefit from having a larger market to sell to. Microsoft will be able to market its products across the world and benefit from the sales revenue generated by overseas sales. It will also be able to capitalise on expanding markets, particularly in developing countries. The higher sales generated by selling overseas will also allow Microsoft to benefit from economies of scale.

7 The business environment is a dynamic one and it is vital that a company like Microsoft manages its business effectively in response to changes in the environment. Management of change can be broken down into two types, foreseeable and unforseeable change.

Foreseeable change is one that can be planned for by the organisation. For example, as Microsoft grows in size it will need to hire new staff and buy more inputs from its suppliers. This will have implications for the amount of cash the business will have. Microsoft needs to plan carefully its future use of resources to manage this change effectively.

Unforeseeable change is that which managers are unable to anticipate and react to. An example of this could be changes in economic activity that occur when the economy grows or is in recession. Microsoft, which produces products that are responsive to changes in incomes would be affected by changes in economic activity. It could also result from breakthroughs in technology in IT. The development of the pentium chip had a dramatic effect on PCs and the software that could be used on them. These changes can be managed effectively by careful forecasting and making predictions about how they will affect Microsoft. The company will need to plan carefully the new software it will need to design to meet the demands of the new Pentium PCs.

Microsoft's ability to manage both foreseeable and unforseeable change is absolutely vital to its survival as a company. In the short term, mistakes made in response to forseeable change will affect both its efficiency and profitability. If sales are increasing and the company fails to hire enough staff to meet this increase in sales then the shortage of workers will put incredible pressure on existing workers who will not work as effectively.

In the long run, Microsoft's ability to react to unforseeable change is critical. If it cannot react to changes in technology and the economic environment then the company may not be able to survive (for example, if a new product replaces Microsoft technology). Thus it is vital that the company's management are in a good position to respond to the changes through careful planning and forecasting.

UNIT 2 *Organisational objectives*

LEVI – A COMFORTABLE FIT

Student book pages 23–25

1 a The 'mission statement' sets out the overall objective of an organisation. Part of Levi's mission statement is to create an 'empowered company'. The mission statement is made clear to the whole organisation, along with its external stakeholders. The statement is made to give the organisation focus which should help decision making. For example, the managers of Levi should be clear about what they are trying to achieve at Levi and enable them to assess performance in terms of whether the mission is being achieved.

b The long term direction of an organisation is determined by the decision making that takes place in the present and the future. For example, Levi's decision to go back to its traditional 501 jean and concentrate on denim products could have been led by its mission statement. Without a mission statement, the focus for its decision making would not be as clear.

c The problem with mission statements is that they can be expressed in a vague manner, which means they do not offer a focus that gives decision making a precise direction. For example, what is actually meant by the term Levi's objective of 'empowerment'. The objective of improving communication, behaviour and diversity, may not give the organisation anything tangible to work towards. It is important that the mission statement is clear and easy to understand, if it is to be an effective guide to long term decision making.

2 a More power can be given to Levi's employees in the following ways:

- Encouraging workers to become more involved in decision making. This can be done through workers being represented in management meetings.
- Workers can be organised into teams which can offer suggestions on how things can be improved. The Japanese call these teams 'quality circles'.
- Workers can be given more power by allowing them to take a financial stake in the organisation in the form of shares.
- The organisation of the production line can be given over to the workforce who will have responsibility to set it out.

b There are a number of advantages to allowing Levi's work force to have some control over decision making.

- Workers who have more control over their work and a greater say in decision making are likely to have greater motivation. The work of Elton Mayo, Abraham Maslow and Douglas Mcgregor suggested that workers who are more involved in the decision making process will have greater morale and motivation. Better motivated workers are likely to be more productive.
- The workforce are often the closest people to the production of the product and the final consumer. This information puts them in a very good position to advise managers and improve the quality of decision making. Workers on Levi's production line will be in the best position to understand and improve production.

The disadvantages for Levi are:

- The decision making process takes longer with more people involved. Levi's decision making flexibility is reduced with more workers involved.
- Decision making needs to be focused. If Levi has more people involved in the process then decisions taken may not have the precise direction required.

3 **a** A limited company is one where the shareholders enjoy the protection of limited liability. If the company goes bankrupt, the owners will only be liable to pay debts up to the value of their investment. They have a share capital of less then £50,000 and invite individuals to become shareholders as opposed to selling shares through the stock market. Public companies issue shares through the stock exchange and have no real control over who becomes shareholder. These companies have a share capital of above £50,000. In 1984 Levi was a public company in the United States, but in 1985 it was bought back into private ownership by Bob Haas, who was a member of the Levi family. There are differences slight differences in the characteristics of private and public companies in the UK compared to the USA, but the basic principle of private and public companies is the same in the USA.
b Bob Haus spent $1.65 billion on buying back shares that had been issued to the public. This makes him the majority shareholder.
c The advantages to of being a private company are:

- **Private companies allow the existing shareholders to retain control over the organisation.** This would have been important to Bob Haas who wanted to change the direction of Levi and take it back to its core business, denim. He also wanted to change the way the company operated by implementing new Japanese management techniques. These changes may not have been possible with opposition from the shareholders who would have been involved if Levi was a public company.

- **Private companies are normally smaller than public companies.** They do not suffer as much from diseconomies of scale that affect huge public companies. To a certain extent Levi slimmed down its operation when it became a private company, returning to its core business. This allowed the business to specialise on what it was traditionally good at doing, making jeans and leaving activities that they are not as specialised in, such as ski wear.

The disadvantages of being a private company are:

- **The loss of access to additional finance that may be needed by the company.** Bob Haas had to borrow the money to buy back the shares, this would have incurred substantial interest payments in the future. The company would not have the option of issuing new shares through the stock market to raise additional funds.

- **They do not benefit from the economies of scale that public companies do because private companies are generally smaller than public companies.** By slimming down its operations Levi will not have the benefits of risk being spread into other products.

The key here for Levi is the control needed by Bob Haas to introduce the change in direction in terms of products and management style. These changes would have been difficult for Levi as a public company because shareholders could have opposed this. In the short run, the buy back was expensive, but in the long run it gave Levis the opportunity to achieve greater success.

ORGANISATIONAL OBJECTIVES

THE FITNESS PLANT SETS STRATEGIC OBJECTIVES

Student book pages 25–26

1 The hierarchy of objectives is the structure of objectives that an organisation needs to achieve in order to achieve its overall mission. In the case of the Fitness Plant, it has set a itself a mission of 'giving its members the best possible environment to achieve their own personal fitness goals'.

In order to achieve this, the Fitness Plant has set itself a number of long term objectives. This includes; 'training new and existing staff in all the latest fitness techniques', as well as 'keeping the club's equipment as up to date as any fitness club in the country'. Once it has set its long term objectives, the club would need to set short objectives, such as setting up training courses for its staff so that they can make sure they are trained in the latest fitness techniques, as well as assessing the current state of fitness equipment to see whether it is up to date. Individual departments within the Fitness Plant need to set their own objectives, for example the swimming centre would need to make sure that its staff are set the objective of being trained to the highest standards. Finally, the tactics and strategies that need to be employed by the Fitness Plant to achieve its short and long term objectives. A series of training programmes set up to train staff would be used to reach the goal of highly trained staff.

Only by achieving each objective within the hierarchy can the Fitness Plant achieve its overall mission.

2 a Total Quality Management (TQM) involves the setting of the goal of quality to each area of the organisation, so that the whole organisation achieves the highest quality in the provision of its good or service. Each department within the Fitness Plant should be looking to deliver quality in its operations. TQM is a customer led objective, which means maximising the satisfaction of the consumers of the product. Through its mission statement – 'giving its members the best possible environment to achieve their own personal fitness goals', the Fitness Plant has shown its commitment to TQM by focusing on the consumer.

b The employment of Total Quality Management will affect profitability in both the long and the short term. In the short term, as is made clear by the company's finance director, profits may fall. This is because the cost of implementing TQM is high. Updating machinery, training employees, is not a cheap process. It is unlikely to create new business straight away; revenue will not be increased, but costs will rise, reducing profits. However, if the product being produced by the Fitness Plant is improved then the company may well attract new business in the long run, which could increase revenues and profits. The company may also strengthen loyalty to its business from consumers, allowing it to increase prices and profits. This may well be the case if it brings in a wealthier customer who is attracted by the standards the Fitness Plant has achieved.

3 The swimming centre has worked towards its own objectives which could have the following advantages:

- If the manager and team that work in the fitness centre achieve their own objectives successfully then that area of the business will attract consumers to the Fitness Plant. The publicity gained through attracting celebrities may well benefit the whole organisation.
- The swimming centre may well give a lead to other departments at the Fitness Plant who will compete for the same success. Their improved

performance will help the whole performance of the Fitness Plant in achieving its mission.

However, there are disadvantages of one department working towards its own objectives:

- By working towards its own objectives the swimming centre may not necessarily be in line with the objectives of the whole organisation. There may well be a conflict of objectives between the Fitness Plant and the swimming department. This conflict could cause management problems between the swimming centre manager, David Elstob and the senior managers. Without the freedom to manage, David Elstob may lose motivation. If the swimming centre does not follow the objectives set by senior managers it may not achieve its overall mission.
- It could also mean that resent builds up in other departments who see that the swimming centre is working towards its own objectives. This could adversely affect morale within the company.

The key point seems to be that if the Fitness Plant wants to achieve its mission it will probably need the swimming centre to follow the mission and objectives set for the whole organisation rather than its own objectives. This will probably mean some skilful management on the part of Andrew Elms, the company's managing director.

4 a Andrew Elms has made the following mistakes in trying to implement the new development plan:

- Andrew Elms has failed to involve his staff in the plan that has been drawn up. Because people have had no input in the decision making process which produced the plan there will inevitably be some resentment amongst the staff. This could lead to a fall in morale and the implementation of the plan could fail on this basis. For example, by not involving the finance director, Helen Aspen, an assessment of the cost of the proposals may not have been made accurately.
- By not involving the staff, Elms will have missed out on a valuable input in the decision making process. His staff will know almost better than anyone what is achievable and what is not.
- Elms has presented the plan without any time for the workforce or shareholders to respond to his proposals. Again, this could lead to resentment and a fall in morale.
- The shareholders have not received any consultation on the plan. This could lead to problems, as shareholders who are unhappy about the plan could refuse to sanction its implementation.
- There is no attempt to involve the consumers in the development of the organisation.

b The Development Plan

Implementation of the Fitness Plant's development plan

To: The Directors of the fitness plant

The aim of this report is to suggest ways in which the new development plan can be implemented successfully.

Consultation

1 Consultation with staff
   It is crucial that the whole workforce has some input into the development plan. All staff should be circulated with the questionnaire which asks them about how they think the organisation should develop over the next 10 years. They should be asked to give specific information on their area within the organisation.

2 Consultation with consumers
   It is important that the consumers (members) of the fitness plan are asked about their feelings on how the organisation could change. This could be done through a customer questionnaire.

3 Consultation with shareholders
   The shareholders should be given a questionnaire to see what their views are on how the fitness plant could develop.

Drawing up the plan

1 The committee
   A committee should be formed which has the responsibility of producing a draft plan. Andrew Elms should head the committee which would include department managers. The group should be large enough to contribute to a pool of ideas, but not too large that it hinders the production of the plan.

2 Producing the draft
   It is important that the committee considers the ideas put forward by all the stakeholders in the fitness plant. A draft plan should be drawn up based on the ideas put forward.

Review

The draft plan should be published and circulated amongst all the employees and shareholders. There should also be some sampling of the views of Fitness Factory's members to gauge their reaction to the changes that could be made. However, the draft should only go to employees and shareholders.

The employees and shareholders should be given a one month time period to submit their comments on the plan to the committee.

The comments made by each group of stakeholders should be taken on board by the committee who will then produce a final draft.

UNIT 3

The internal organisation of business

THE RESTRUCTURING OF THE HUNTER GROUP

Student book pages 40–43

1 a Organisation by function means that the structure of the organisation is based on the business functions production, marketing, finance and human resources. The Hunter Group is currently organised on a functional basis with each line in its hierarchy based on a particular function. For example, the sales director heads the sales function; the group sales manager is answerable to the sales director, and the factory sales manager is answerable to the group sales manager.

b The span of control is a measurement of the number of people who are responsible to a given individual in a business. The factory sales manager at Hunters has four area sales managers, as well as a sales office manager, that are directly responsible to him. This gives the factory sales manager a span of control of five.

c A decentralised structure is a management structure where the authority of management is dispersed to lower levels of an organisation. The management consultant's report on Hunters recommended that decision making within the company is decentralised. Under the new organisational framework, managers within each product area will have greater responsibility to make decisions which have been delegated to them from director level.

d An organisation chart sets out the formal structure of the organisation in terms of how individuals and departments are linked together using the principal lines of authority. It sets out what an individual's responsibility is within the organisation's structure and who the individual is answerable to. In the new organisation chart drawn up by Hunters it can be seen that the Passenger Jet Manager is responsible for the decision making in the passenger jet division. This manager is responsible to board of directors for the decisions they have taken. The organisation chart allows individuals within the organisation to see where they fit into the organisation.

e Quality circles are small groups of workers (five to ten people) who meet on a voluntary basis in order to consider ways of improving quality and productivity in their work areas. They originated in Japan and they have taken on growing importance in organisations worldwide. The development plan employed by Hunters will involve the use of quality circles as the company strives to improve its performance. Quality circles give workers a greater say in decision making which may improve moral and raise their motivation. Workers know the production system better than anyone and are thus able to pinpoint problems as well put forward ways that production can be improved.

2 Organisation by function has the following advantages:

- A functional structure is a logical way to break up a business and it is understood by everyone. The managers and workforce at Hunters will clearly see and understand their position in a hierarchy that is organised in this way. Workers and managers who understand their position and responsibility will feel more

comfortable and will be better motivated.
- Functional structuring allows for specialisation in specific departmental areas. This allows workers and managers to develop expertise in their function and become more effective at their jobs. If this happens throughout the organisation the whole organisation will become more effective. Hunters see workers and managers gain expertise and attain greater efficiency in production, sales and marketing by specialising in specific functions.
- Functional organisation avoids duplication of effort. The managers and workers at Hunters have specific functional tasks such as production and finance. For example, functional organisation at Hunters would avoid the problem of marketing activities by the passenger jet division being duplicated by the light aircraft division.
- Training will carried out by departmental specialists in a functionally organised organisation. At Hunters the specialist training provided by the finance division may well be better that training given on finance within the light aircraft division.

Organisation by product has the following advantages:

- Functional organisation can mean that the individual functions within the organisation are too inward looking, and may put their own aims above those of the whole organisation. At Hunters, for example, the finance division may push for lower and lower unit costs which is at odds with the production division which is interested in the quality of the product they produce. In a product organisation, functions are combined within a product area and there is less likely to be a conflict between divisions that reduces the effectiveness of the organisation. In fact, product organisation can lead to healthy competition between the different product groups which can enhance the performance of the organisation. At Hunters, competition between the light aircraft division and passenger jet division could enhance the company's performance.
- Product organisation allows Hunters' directors to delegate responsibility to its divisions more easily than when it was organised by function. Unlike functional organisations where delegation is difficult because the decisions taken by one area have huge implications for other areas, product organisation allows for greater autonomy. At present a finance decision has a major implication for all other areas of Hunters so it is risky to delegate it. However, decisions taken by the passenger jet division have far less impact on the other divisions.
- Product organisation allow divisions to specialise in their own product area. The division gains increased knowledge of its market and customers. The helicopter division will be able gain more specialist market knowledge and understanding if Hunters organises itself on a product basis.
- Product organisation means that the directors will be able to measure the effectiveness of each division more efficiently because they will be generating costs, revenues and profits. These figures can perhaps be used to measure performance more effectively than, say, the costs of the production function being compared to the revenues of the sales function.

Product organisation tends to work most effectively in large businesses which have a range of product lines. Hunters is a large organisation which can most effectively divide itself up by product division along the lines of its passenger jet, light aircraft, military aircraft and helicopter divisions. The key benefit is that the divisions will be able to specialise in their specific product areas and competition between divisions will work to Hunters' advantage as opposed to its disadvantage when it was organised on a functional basis.

3 When the new divisions are set up managers will be appointed to head the divisions and take responsibility for running them. A great deal of decision making will be delegated from the board of directors to these divisional managers. The managers will have to be able to cope with the responsibility and decision making delegated to them. The managers must be able to accept the decision delegated to them and implement the decision effectively.

The managers appointed should have the following characteristics:

- A sound understanding of the market the business is selling to and the customers Hunters is serving.
- A sound understanding of the division they will be heading, and the systems that operate within it.
- An ability to lead people effectively and motivate staff.
- Effective communication skills, so that decisions can be clearly communicated to the workforce as well as the directors to whom they are answerable.
- The ability to delegate decisions to subordinates. This will be very important with the manager heading up such a large area within the business.
- The ability to manage their own workload effectively.
- The ability to plan effectively and see new opportunities for the division to exploit.

The managers appointed should have all these characteristics, although different managers will have differing strengths. The question that will face Hunters is whether to choose managers from within the company or to appoint external managers. Internal candidates will have the knowledge and understanding of the business and the market, but may lack the new ideas needed to take advantage of new opportunities presented by the restructuring. Candidates from outside the business may well be able to give the new ideas and direction needed by Hunters.

4 Kaizen programmes and groups mean employing Japanese management techniques to improve production efficiency. Workers are encouraged to assess their own roles and performance through quality circles, management meetings and suggestion schemes. The process is designed to bring about continuous improvement in production without the major changes in production. In the passenger jet division of Hunters, workers could be asked to consider their own work to see how it might be improved. This could bring about the following benefits:

- Continuous improvement in production will lead to an improvement in the quality of the final product produced by Hunters.
- Greater production efficiency will reduce waste and, ultimately, the unit costs of production. This may allow Hunters to reduce prices.
- The process of Kaizen will increase worker participation in the decision making process which could improve worker motivation.
- The process of worker participation will improve the relationship between workers and managers at Hunters which will improve the quality of management.

In the long term, these improvements may well increase profitability as greater efficiency reduces costs, and the quality of the product improves which could increase sales.

5 a The changes that Hunters want to introduce to the company will mean a major upheaval for the whole organisation. This will bring about the following difficulties for Hunters:

- The workforce are unhappy about such a huge change to the way they work, as well as the redundancies that will arise from the changes. There is already the threat of industrial action from the engineering union.
- The changes in working practices will be difficult to implement because the workforce will be used to one way of working and changing this will not be easy for them.
- The changes in organisational structure mean that middle managers will be made redundant as many management posts are removed. This will bring about resistance from managers who will naturally resist the change.
- The directors are reluctant to change because many have worked with the company in one way for 20 years. If they are reluctant to change then this discontent will filter through to the rest of the workforce.
- There will be logistical difficulties in reorganising the company; production plant, offices, lines of distribution, etc., will all need to be changed.
- The difficulties identified will concern the shareholders who will worry about how the changes which are due to take place may affect their investment.
- The changes may also make external stakeholders in the business nervous. Banks, suppliers, and customers will all have concerns about the changes because of the impact it may have on their businesses. A strike, for example, could mean an interruption to the supply of Hunters' customers.

The key problem in the short term for Hunters will be the reluctance of both the managers and workers at Hunters to change. This is the key aspect that Hunters needs to manage for successful change to take place.

   b The structural changes that have been set out by the management consultants could be introduced in three ways:

- The management can force through changes with little consultation from the workforce. Hunters would make sure that they clearly communicate the changes that are going to take place and why they taking place, but offer little or no opportunity for input from the workforce. A time-scale will be set and the changes implemented in that time-scale. The advantages of doing it this way is that the changes the company believes need to be made will be put into place without any watering down, which may reduce the effectiveness of the changes. The process will be a quick one, assuming everything goes to plan. The change will also be clear to everyone particularly external stakeholders and shareholders who will know exactly where the company is going. The major disadvantages are that the changes will meet resistance which could prevent the successful implementation of the restructuring. Once the restructuring has been implemented, its successful operation will be dependent on the efforts of the workforce which may not be forthcoming if the changes are forced through.
- The management could introduce the changes through effective consultation with the workforce and management. Input from the workforce could be invited and their suggestions taken on board. This method is more likely to gain the acceptance of the workforce and make the change successful. Once the changes are in place, the workforce are more likely to make the restructuring work. The workforce may come up with ideas of their own which will improve the restructuring. However, the process of restructuring will be much slower. The outcome may mean that the plans are watered down and not as effective as the original draft. If the restructuring changes then external stakeholders will not be able to see the changes as clearly

which could undermine their confidence in the company.
- The management could try to implement a strategy falling somewhere between the first two options with some limited consultation with the workforce. This could give the advantages of both options and reduce their disadvantages. However, it is difficult to judge where to draw the line on employee input. Too little input will still bring about resentment and too much will slow the whole process down.

This major change at Hunters will be a painful one for the company but it is critical for the company's long term survival. Forcing through the change, despite its obvious disadvantages, may well be the only way of giving the new structure a clear direction and a good chance of success.

MANAGING FUTURE SUCCESS AT DIXONS

Student book pages 43–44

1   a The Kingfisher group owns the following retail chains: Darty, Woolworths, Comet, B&Q and Superdrug.

b There are a number of reasons why Dixons has different names for its chains of stores:

- Dixons has its own brand image and sells products that fit with this image. Customers think of televisions, HIFI, cameras, and videos: home entertainment products. People do not associate Dixons with white goods such as fridges and dishwashers. If all the stores owned by Dixons were under the same name it would weaken the Dixons brand.
- By operating under different store names Dixons can target individual market segments more effectively. For example, the target market of PC World will be perhaps more knowledgeable about computers than the people Currys targets to sell computers to.
- Customers are given the impression that they have greater choice by the variety of store names than if Dixons sold under one name. A customer looking for a video may well go to Dixons and then to Currys to compare products. They would not do this between two Dixons stores and would instead turn to an alternative company such as Comet. This will increase the sales of the Dixons group as a whole.

2   a A bureaucratic organisation is one where there is a strictly formal pyramid hierarchy with strong control from the senior management that is passed down through successive layers through a formal decision making process. It involves a great deal of paper-based checks on decisions and actions. A non-bureaucratic organisation, such as Dixons, has the following characteristics:

- A flat organisation chart with a reduced number of levels in the organisation's hierarchy. Dixons has a relatively flat organisation chart.
- Delegated decision making. This is the case with many major decisions delegated by the board of directors down to the individual store groups.
- A structure that encourages two-way communication between managers and their subordinates.
- A wide span of control exists with managers having a large number of subordinates reporting to them.

b The following factors will constrain the ability of an organisation to respond to change:

- Weak management that struggles to redirect the business. The senior management that have control over the overall direction of the company must be able to redirect the company quickly and easily. Henri Fayol (1841–1925) identified management ability to command and organise the business to bring about effective change. To a large extent management's ability to do this is based on their effectiveness as leaders. If the leadership is ineffective and weak it will not be able to respond to change. Dixons, however, has the direction at the senior management level to do this.

- The structure of the organisation affects its ability to change. If the structure is rigid and bureaucratic it may not be able to quickly respond to change. Dixons is non-bureacratic which makes it responsive to change.
- The flexibility of the workforce will constrain the ability of the organisation to change. If the workforce lacks flexibility because the workers do not have high enough skills or because they have not been given enough responsibility in the past and are as a result only used to one way of working, then the organisation will be sluggish to respond to change. Through effective training and delegation of decision making Dixons has the ability to respond quickly to change.

Because technology in the products that Dixons retails is changing so fast, it is essential for the company to respond quickly to change. The structure, management and workforce of Dixons allows it to do this.

3 **a** The span of control is the number of subordinates that are directly responsible to a manager. If the manager has a large number of subordinates responsible to him then the span of control is wide; if the number of subordinates responsible to the manager is small then the span of control is narrow.

b Dixons management is likely to have a wide span of control because the organisation chart is relatively flat. Dixons has an organisation structure where many decisions are delegated. A Dixons store manager is responsible for the day to day decision making that is involved in running the store. This means that they will have a number of store staff that are directly to responsible to them, giving them a wide span of control. The organisation chart for a Dixons store could look like Figure 1.

c There are a number of factors that determine the span of control of a Dixons store manager.

- The calibre and ability of the manager. The greater the ability of the manager in terms of managing groups of people the wider the span of control will be. Good managers will be offered larger stores to manage, which gives them a wider span of control.

Figure 1 The organisation chart for a Dixons store

- The quality of the people being controlled will have a bearing on the span of control. The more motivated and able workers are, the easier it is to control them which allows for a broader span. If Dixons appoints good staff, the span of control can be wide for an individual manager.
- The nature of the task is important in determining the span of control. The more crucial the task is to the organisation the narrower the span of control will be. Because the task of managing stores is so critical to Dixons the span of control of managers is limited. This accounts for the use of section managers who control the shop assistants within their stores.
- Company policy will have a bearing on the span of control. Dixons likes to delegate decision making to store level which broadens the span of control of the individual store managers.

Probably the most critical influence within a Dixons store will be the size of the store and the number of people it employs. Larger stores will offer managers wider spans of control, although a large store is likely to employ more section managers.

UNIT 4
Information and business decision making

RELAUNCHING THE POLO

Student book pages 67–68

1 a There are four different market research techniques that Nestlé could have used:

- **Personal interviews.** In a market research project, this is where individuals within a target population are interviewed by market researchers representing Nestlé to gain information about their views on the organisation, its products and the market. This would normally take the form of an interviewer asking questions from a questionnaire.
- **Panel interviews.** Here the interviewer representing Nestlé would interview a group of people as opposed to an individual. The interviewer would work from a questionnaire asking questions of the group. In the group discussion, the interaction of the panel of respondents can provide more information than a personal interview.
- **Telephone survey.** In a telephone survey, the interview takes place over the telephone using a prepared questionnaire.
- **Postal survey.** In this case, the market research questionnaires that Nestlé have produced are sent through the post so that the respondent can complete the questionnaire in their own time.

Each type of survey is an option to Nestlé and their decision on which one to use would be based on factors such as; funds it has available, the size sample needed, the speed of response required and the desired response rate.

b I would have chosen the panel interview as their method of market research because:

- Nestlé is a major multinational company, so the relatively high cost of a panel discussion compared to telephone and postal surveys would not be the constraint it would be for smaller organisations.
- Because Nestlé is looking to change direction with the Polo it would need detailed, accurate views from the respondents of the survey and, because of the complex nature of the question that would be asked, an interviewer would need to be present to guide the respondents.
- I have chosen a panel as opposed to a personal interview because such a major change in direction needs new ideas; the new ideas thrown up in a group discussion could be useful to Nestlé.

2 a Sampling is the selection of a group of individuals from a population, who will be used as part of a market research survey. For example, the target population for Nestlé would be the broad group of people that consume mints. A sample would be a group of 2,000 chosen from within the population whose views would represent those of the population. Sampling has to be used because it would be too expensive and impractical to survey every person in a market, particularly a broad one, such as people who consume mints. Sampling can be random; where every person in the target population has an equal chance of being surveyed. There is also a quota sample, where specific individuals are chosen so that the sample reflects the type of people who consume the product. For example, if 70% of mint consumers are men then 70% of the sample must be men.

b Random sampling has the advantage of providing the most statistically accurate data with a relatively small sampling error. A quota sample, on the other hand, is not as statistically accurate because the data can be distorted by the choice of sample. If Nestlé try to sample 70% of men because they think this is the proportion of men who consume their product then the choice of men could produce a statistical bias. This is because the men chosen may give a series of views that do not accurately reflect those of the target population.

Quota sampling has the advantage of being a more cost effective way of sampling the population than random sampling. A random sample may well involve very large groups to make it representative of the entire population. A quota sample where specific categories of people are targeted to represent the population could be carried out by sampling 1,000 people. The same cross section of people using random sampling may mean choosing 5,000 people. A truly random sample would involve Nestlé sampling at different times during the day because one carried out at that time would miss out on working people. Thus it can be seen that the quota sample produces results at a much lower cost.

It is possible to break up the population into groups and then carry out a random sample. This offers greater statistical accuracy than a quota sample, but it does so at a lower cost. For example, the population can be broken up into different strata based on age, sex, or socio-economic grouping. A random sample can then be carried out within these strata. Nestlé could break up its mint customers into groupings based on these strata. Alternatively, it could random sample a cluster of the population which again offers the statistical accuracy of a random sample at a lower cost.

3 a A good questionnaire is one that provides the information which allows the organisation to achieve its objective from the market research. The questionnaires used by Nestlé should allow it to achieve its market research objective, which is to establish the reasons behind Polo's decline in market share. Each question in the questionnaire must contribute to achieving the overall objective of the research. It is important that the questions are not biased towards a particular response and that they are easy for the respondent to understand. The questions should also provide responses that are easy to interpret.
b Here is a selection of questions Nestlé could have used:

Sample Nestlé questionnaire

1 Circle the age category that you are in:
12–17   18–23   24–34   35–45   46–56
57–67   68+

2 Are you male or female?   male ☐
                            female ☐

Note: These first two questions tell Nestlé the demographic market segment that the people who are answering questions fall into. They are vital to Nestlé because they identify how different segments within their market are reacting to different products and changes that are taking place in the market. For example, the finding that spearmint flavour has growing popularity in the youth market can only be established through these two questions.

3 For each of the following types of mint, rate how much you like or dislike the mint:

INFORMATION AND BUSINESS DECISION MAKING

▶▶

	like a lot	like	no preference	dislike	dislike a lot
Strong mints					
Spearmints					
Softmints					
Sugar free mints					

Note: This question tells Nestlé what type of mints people prefer. This is important in terms of broadening Polo's product mix to include different types of mint. It is clear from the case study that there is growing demand in the youth market for spearmint flavour and strong mints in the adult market.

4 **a** Pie charts to illustrate market share % in the mint market.
b Pie charts are an effective way of representing the data produced by a market research survey. In this case the market share accounted for by different products in the mint market can be clearly represented using pie charts. Graphical representations of this type are particularly good at communicating information to managers who have to make decisions based on the data. Managers at Nestlé will clearly be able to see how Polo's market share compares to other products in the market, information that clearly communicates that action will need to be taken. The charts can be used by managers to support the decisions they might want to make through some form of presentation. Pie charts are particularly effective when it comes to showing proportions that arise from market research as opposed to situations where managers are looking at totals. The weakness of pie charts is that they fail to show how data changes over time when there is only small changes in that data. In this case, the changing shares of Polo relative to other mints are difficult to spot.

5 Even with extensive market research there have been some spectacular product failures. Some classic examples include: new taste Coca Cola and Levi suits. In both cases, despite extensive market research, these products failed. The reason for the failures was that consumers did not respond as managers, led by market research, thought they would do.

There are a number of factors that can account for these difficulties:

● Consumers do not always act in reality in the way that they do under market research conditions. For example, young people in the 16–24 age group may in the research show a preference for spearmint, but do not show the same kind of preference when it comes to actually buying the product.
● There is often an element of bias in market research that makes the findings inaccurate. This bias could emerge from the type of questions set in a questionnaire, or in the way the interviewer presents the questionnaire to the respondents. The finding that sugar free mints have a female bias may have arisen because of stereotyping of female preferences. The interviewer

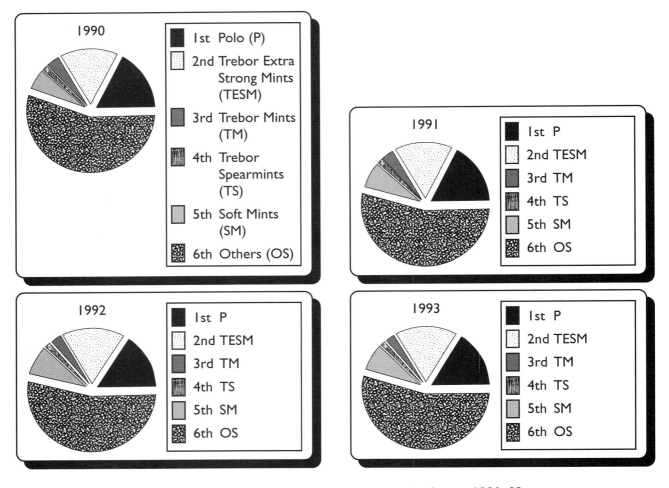

Figure 2 Pie charts to show the market share of different brands of mint, 1990–93

could have led women into the sugar free response in a personal interview.
- There is always the chance of a sampling error distorting the results of a survey because the sample chosen is not truly representative of the target population. This could happen with a quota sample which is not as statistically accurate as a random sample. An overemphasis on young people chosen in the Nestlé sample could well produce results that do not reflect the views of a truly representative group of Polo consumers.
- Market researchers may simply misinterpret the results of a survey and draw conclusions that cannot really be drawn from the data. The view that Polo is a predictable brand that has not been developed is viewed by Nestlé as a negative thing that needs to be changed. However, the predictability of Polo could be interpreted as its strength.

Whilst there are a number problems associated with research, making crucial marketing decisions without research is considerably more risky. Market research allows the organisation to look at how the consumer is thinking and how they might react to new products or changes to existing products. Without research Nestlé would have only anecdotal evidence to go on when it analyses why its market share is falling and how it could try to prevent such a fall.

PROMOTING ASPEN'S COMMUNICATIONS EQUIPMENT

1 a

Figure 3 Monthly sales figures for Aspen Communications, April 1997 to April 1998

b, c

Month	Sales £m	4 quarter total £m	8 quarter total £m	Trend £m
Apr 97	3.25			
May	3.11			
June	3.46	13.37	26.83	3.35
July	3.55	13.46	27.35	3.42
Aug	3.34	13.89	28.21	3.53
Sept	3.54	14.32	28.32	3.54
Oct	3.89	14.00	28.54	3.57
Nov	3.23	14.54	29.30	3.66
Dec	3.88	14.76	29.40	3.68
Jan 98	3.76	14.64	29.25	3.66
Feb	3.77	14.61		
Mar	3.20			

Table 6 The four point moving average sales are plotted in Figure 3 ×—×

d The moving average that has been calculated and plotted on the graph in Figure 3 shows that the moving average sales figure has risen over the 12 months since the promotional campaign was put into place. Basing the success of the campaign on the sales figure, this would suggest that the campaign had been a success.

e Basing the campaign's success or failure purely on sales figures could be a mistake. A number of other factors also need to be taken into account:

- The activity in the market. The market for communication equipment could be expanding which would account for the rise in sales.
- The activity in the economy. The economy could be expanding which would account for the rise in sales.
- The price of the product could have fallen which would have accounted for the rise in sales.
- The quality of the product produced by Aspen could have improved which would have accounted for the rise in sales.

2 a Arithmetic mean £41.98m/12
$$= £3.5m$$

Median £3.46 + £3.54/2 = £3.5

b £3.5m/1.15 = £3.04m

3 There are a number of ways the promotional campaign could assessed:

- The sales figures, which have already been looked at, could be used. Using Sarah Miles' figures, it can be seen that a 20% rise in marketing budget has led to a 15% rise in sales. If the costs of the promotional campaign are subtracted from the extra sales generated the profit generated from the promotional campaign can be calculated.
- Market research could be used to assess the effectiveness of the campaign. This could take the form of a short questionnaire that is put to customers on how they had heard of Aspen and why they had chosen to buy the company's products.

- The sales force could be questioned on how successful they believed the promotional campaign to be. This is because the sales force is close to the customer and will receive feedback from customers on their views of the campaign.

To really assess the success or failure of the campaign it needs to be judged against the objectives of the campaign. Sarah Miles has set out to change the image of Aspen. In the short term, sales would be one measure of success, but the benefits of a change of image would only be felt in the long term. Continuous market research of customer views on the company's image over the long term would be the best way measuring the success of the promotional campaign.

UNIT 5
Financial accounting – Section A: Accounting and finance

THE AUDIT OF FOCUS 2000

Student book page 91

1 Focus 2000 balance sheet 31/12/98

Fixed assets	£'000
Buildings	350
Plant & Machinery	400
Vehicles	170
Fixtures	180
Patents	150
Investments	400
	1,650
Current assets	
Stock	300
Debtors	280
Cash	240
	820
Current liabilities	
Creditors	400
Tax payable	120
Overdraft	190
	710
Working capital	110
Net assets	1,760
Shareholders funds	
Ordinary shares	400
Retained profit	210
Revaluations	250
General reserves	200
	1,060
Long-term liabilities	
Debentures	500
Mortgage	200
	700
	1,760

Table 7 Focus 2000 balance sheet

2 Focus 2000 profit and loss account year ending 31st December 1998

Sales £'000		2,100
Opening stock 1/1/98	200	
Purchases	600	
	800	
Less closing stock	300	
Cost of sales	500	
Wages	200	
Direct costs		700
Gross trading profit		1,400
Overheads	210	
Administration	120	
Depreciation	300	
Marketing costs	100	
Indirect costs		730
Net trading profit		70
Interest and dividend received	80	
Interest paid	90	
Net interest expense		10
Net profit before tax		660
Tax 30%		198
Net profit after tax		462
Dividends 60%		277.2
Retained profit		184.8

Table 8 Focus 2000 profit and loss account

3 The following users would be interested in Focus' accounts:

- shareholders
- employees
- the local community
- the government
- tax authorities
- other organisations
- bank and other creditors.

4 The following could be the interests of three of the users of Focus 2000 accounts:

- The shareholders, as well as potential shareholders, will be interested in financial information that will affect their investment.

Profitability will be particularly important, but perhaps more precisely it will be after tax profit and the amount that is to be distributed to the shareholders in the form of dividends.
- The banks and other creditors will be interested in the ability of the company they have leant money to, to pay them back. The amount of cash that Focus has will determine the company's ability to pay its debts. Thus banks and creditors will look at the amount of cash working capital in Focus' balance sheet.
- Focus' employees will be concerned with their job security and how much pay they can negotiate for. The amount of cash that Focus has and its profitability will be of particular interest to them.

FORTUNA EDUCATION RECONSIDER PRODUCTION IN CHINA

Student book pages 92–93

1
a A private limited company is normally a small medium sized business, although some are large (Virgin Group), that are not listed on the stock exchange. Fortuna is an example of a medium sized private limited company. They are often family run businesses where shareholders are invited to buy shares in the company. They have limited liability (hence the term limited after the name) which means that if the business goes bankrupt the amount paid to the creditors of the business is limited to the assets of the company and is not the liability of the shareholders personally.
b A debenture is a unit of debt sold by a company which is a long term loan made to the company by the buyer. Normally, they are fixed interest rate loans made over a set period of time when they are bought back by the company. Debentures can be secured against an asset, such as property or land. Over half of Fortuna's long term borrowing in 1996 was through debentures and the finance raised by Fortuna to expand into CDs was raised through a debenture issue.
c Direct labour is a worker whose activity is directly related to the production of the organisation's final product. The direct labour employed by Fortuna would be involved in the production of the tapes, for example the language experts whose voices can be heard on the tapes. Direct labour is a direct cost of production and is subtracted from sales revenue to get gross profit.
d The balance sheet is the financial statement that shows what a company owns in the form of assets and owes in the form of liabilities at a particular point in time. Because of the principle of the accounting equation where each transaction made by an organisation always has a source and use of funds, assets will always equal liabilities and the balance sheet always balances. Fortuna's balance sheet shows that on 31 December 1996 it had net assets of £4.1m which were financed by £4.1m of liabilities.
e The profit and loss account is a financial statement that shows a business's revenues and costs over a financial period. If revenues are greater than costs then the business will record a profit on its activities over the period. It is a statement that would be used by Fortuna's stakeholders to judge the trading success of the business. The profit reported by Fortuna in its profit and loss account has increased in each

year from 1994–96. The account also shows how much corporation tax the company is going to pay and what dividend it will pay to its shareholders.

2 a Reserves are funds that are attributable (owed) to the shareholders of the business. Thus they are included under shareholders funds in the balance sheet. They can split into two types: capital reserves, such as property revaluations, and revenue reserves which is retained profit. On 31 December 1996 Fortuna's reserves stood at £1.45m.
b Fortuna's reserves would have increased from 1994–96 because it is making a profit in each of these years and this profit is being added to the reserves. The profit and loss account shows that Fortuna is earning increasingly higher profits that would be attributable to Fortuna's shareholders. Not all the after tax profit would be retained by the business. Some would be paid to the shareholders as dividends.

3 Fortuna's balance sheet and profit and loss accounts can be used to make the following judgements:

- Sales of Fortuna's products have increased by 128% from 1994 to 1996 whilst direct costs have only increased by 58%, which has led to a 165% increase in gross profits. Indirect costs have increased by 43% which means that net profits have increased by 355%. This large rise in profitability suggests that Fortuna has performed very well over the period which would certainly please the directors of the company.
- The value of Fortuna measured by its net asset value has increased from £2.6m to £4.1m, a rise of 58%. This increase in value is again something that would please directors because it means the value of the company they own has increased.
- The amount of cash in Fortuna's balance sheet has increased by 100% which means that the company's cash position has strengthened.
- Fortuna's long term borrowing has increased by 25% but its shareholders funds has increased by 78%. This means that the proportion of capital employed accounted for by shareholders funds has increased and again this would please the directors.

All these factors suggest the Fortuna's performance has been excellent over the period 1994–96.

4 Fortuna's decision to move production away from the Far East and back to the UK where they will manufacture the tapes themselves may have the following implications for their balance sheet and profit and loss accounts:

- If direct costs rise because it is more expensive to produce the tapes and books in the UK the gross and net profits will fall (assuming prices remain the same) reducing the profit reported in the profit and loss account. However, shipping costs and other administration costs associated with out-sourcing in Asia will be reduced which reduces indirect costs and increases profits. Overall, in the short term, higher direct costs will dominate so profits will fall.
- If profits fall then the growth of the company will be slowed down and the rise in value of the company measured by its net assets will be reduced.
- The decision to produce the tapes and books in UK could mean acquiring machinery, land, buildings and stock which will increase the value of net assets in the balance sheet.
- The value of assets purchased will have to be financed which will increase the value of Fortuna's capital employed. If it is financed through shareholders then shareholders funds will increase in the balance sheet, and if it is financed through borrowing, long term liabilities will increase.

- In the long term, Fortuna's reputation as a company may be enhanced as it is seen as a more ethical organisation. This could increase sales and profits in the profit and loss account.

The key thing the company must weigh up when it is making this decision is whether it wants to reduce its short term profitability in favour of becoming more ethical as an organisation and the possible rise in sales and profits that might bring in the long run.

THE REDBRICK WINE DISTRIBUTORS' BALANCE SHEET

Student book pages 93–94

1 a Creditors are the individuals and companies that an organisation owes money to. Redbrick's trade creditors would be suppliers to the company that Redbrick has not paid at the balance sheet date. Most companies are involved in buying stock on credit so there are always some creditors in the balance sheet. Other creditors could be banks and other lending institutions.
b Ordinary shares represent part ownership in a company. Redbrick has £200,000 of funds provided by ordinary shareholders. Each share that a holder owns represents a unit of ownership in Redbrick. The shareholder has the right to vote at Redbrick's annual general meeting on major items of company policy, including the election of directors to run the company. Ordinary shareholders are paid a dividend which is a proportion of the company's after tax profits.
c Fixed assets are something a business owns. There are permanent assets that are not turned over in the normal course of trading, such as land and buildings. These assets have to be valued at historic cost which means using their purchase price as a basis for their valuation and then subtracting an amount for their depreciation. Redbrick has warehouses, vehicles, computers and fixtures included as part of their tangible fixed assets. Intangible fixed assets are things like trademarks, patents and copyrights owned by the company. There are also financial fixed assets where a company owns shares in another company.

2 The £120,000 profit that Redbrick earned last year is attributable to Redbrick's shareholders as a return on their investment in the company. The process of double entry accounting shows that each time a transaction yields a profit it is included under shareholders funds in the balance sheet. The directors of Redbrick will decide on how much of the after tax profit Redbrick earns will be paid to the shareholders in the form of dividends and how much will be retained in the business. The profit that is retained within the business is included under reserves in the balance sheet; these are called revenue reserves.

3 a Historic cost is the original purchase price of an asset. If Redbrick paid £15,000 for a new machine then this would be the historic cost of the machine. The historic cost is the basis for valuing all assets in the balance sheet and all companies have to follow this principle in the preparation of their balance sheets.
b Historic cost is important in the preparation of the balance sheet because accountants want to use a certain, objective value as a basis for valuing fixed assets. If accountants make a judgement about the possible

market value of an asset then the objectivity of valuation is removed and is open to the interpretation of the valuer. Comparing the value of assets between companies would be very difficult on this basis because assets could be valued in different ways. This would mean that it would be very difficult to compare the balance sheet valuation of assets owned by Redbrick and other companies in the same industry if you were measuring comparative performance. Thus all companies have to follow the principle of historic cost when they are preparing accounts.

4 Because of the principle of realisation, a sale is made when a product is delivered to the customer. It does not matter whether the product sold has been paid for or not. Thus Redbrick's sales revenue and profits remain unchanged despite the fact the cheque for payment has not be received for the goods that redbrick has sold. However, the balance sheet is affected by the non receipt of the cheque. Without payment, the cash value in Redbrick's balance sheet falls by £5,000 and because the £5,000 is now owed to Redbrick the debtors value in the balance sheet rises by £5,000. The current assets section of balance sheet will now look like this:

Current assets	**£'000**
Stock	80
Debtors (+5)	65
Cash (−5)	15
	160

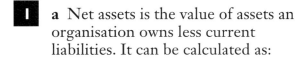

THE SALE OF LAND CRUISER MOTORS LTD

Student book page 94

1 a Net assets is the value of assets an organisation owns less current liabilities. It can be calculated as:

fixed assets + current assets − current liabilities = net assets

Assets are something a business owns. There are permanent assets that are not turned over in the normal course of trading, such as land and buildings. Current assets, on the other hand, are turned over in the normal course of trading and include stock, debtors and cash. Current liabilities are a debt the business owes to a third party and include overdrafts, trade creditors and tax payable.

b For the accountants of Land Cruiser to calculate its value of net assets they need firstly to calculate the value of fixed assets. This means valuing land and buildings, machinery and vehicles, etc. These assets have to be valued at historic cost which means using their purchase price as a basis for their valuation and then subtracting an amount for their depreciation. Land Cruiser would have a forecourt, showrooms, computers and fixtures that would need to be valued in this way. The accountants would also need to assess the value of any tangible fixed assets, such as Land Cruiser's trademark, as well as its financial fixed assets which include shares owned in other companies.

Current assets can be calculated by valuing Land Cruiser's stock which would be in the form of cars. The stock would be valued at historic cost. The amount that is owed to Land Cruiser from its customer's would need to be worked out. Finally the amount of cash the company has would need to be calculated.

Land Cruiser's current liabilities can be worked out by measuring the size of the overdraft, the amount they owe to their suppliers as trade creditors, the amount of tax that is owed to the government and how much dividend is owed to shareholders.

Fixed assets, current assets and current liabilities all have be calculated at a particular point in time.

2 **a** Goodwill is the value of the business over and above the value of its net assets in the balance sheet. It is money value put on the name, reputation and customer base that the company has as a result of its current trading. Land Cruiser has a name as a car dealership and it will have a number of new and regular customers that are attracted by the name and reputation of the company.

b £2m − £1.4m = £0.6m

c Goodwill is written into the balance sheet when a company is being sold and its is included as an intangible fixed asset.

d It is impossible to put an exact figure on Goodwill because the money value on the customer base is a judgement made by the company being sold and agreed by the buyer if they purchase the company. The value of the customer base can change overtime, indeed the change of ownership may adversely affect the customer base. Because of the difficulties of measuring Goodwill it is not seen to be prudent to do and so it is not normally included in a company's balance sheet.

UNIT 5

Financial accounting – Section B Techniques used in the preparation of accounts

BODY CARE CONSIDER AN ATTRACTIVE OFFER

Student book pages 107–108

Note: the figures in the balance sheet are not in '000' as the question suggests.

1 a LIFO and FIFO are accounting techniques used to identify and value stock for entry into the balance sheet and profit and loss accounts.

• FIFO assumes that the first stock to enter the business is the first stock sold. This means that the accountants at Body Care would assume that the stock of moisturising cream that had been in the business the longest would be sold first. This would leave a closing stock valued at the latest price.

• LIFO assumes that the latest stock purchased is the first to be sold. Body Care would be assumed to have sold the moisturising cream at the latest price first which would leave the stock valued at the earliest price as the closing stock.

b

	FIFO	LIFO
opening stock	12,000 @ 1.10 £13,200	12,000 @ 1.10 £13,200
plus purchases		
1 January	25,000 @ 1.10 £27,500	25,000 @ 1.10 £27,500
3 May	30,000 @ 1.20 £36,000	30,000 @ 1.20 £36,000
5 September	38,000 @ 1.25 £47,500	38,000 @ 1.25 £47,500
5 November	15,000 @ 1.28 £19,200	15,000 @ 1.28 £19,200
	120,000 143,400	120,000 143,400
less closing stock		
	15,000 @ 1.28 £19,200	25,000 @ 1.10
	10,000 @ 1.25 £12,500	
	£ 31,700	£ 27,500
cost of sales	£111,700	£115,900

Table 9 The cost of sales using FIFO and LIFO

c The cost of sales figure calculated using FIFO is £111,700 which is less than the £115,900 calculated using LIFO. This means that the profit calculated using LIFO will be less than that calculated using FIFO. Accountants would prefer LIFO because it is more prudent than using FIFO since it reports a lower profit. LIFO also reports a lower value of closing stock than FIFO which is again more prudent. However, this only applies if the price of stock is rising. If its price is falling, FIFO becomes more prudent.

2 a Depreciation is the fall in the value of fixed assets over time. The machinery and vehicles owned by Body Care will all fall in value due to wear and tear and obsolescence. Thus depreciation represents the cost of the fixed asset over time. This cost could be written off (subtracted) from sales revenue when the asset was purchased or when the asset was scrapped at the end of its life. However, subtracting the whole historic cost of the asset at either the year when the asset was purchased or when it was disposed of would understate profits in either of these two years. For example, if Body Care bought a machine for £50,000 and subtracted this amount off in the year of purchase, the profits the company made in that year would be understated. After the purchase year, the machine would go on to produce a stream of revenue throughout its useful life as it was used to produce the company's products. The revenue in future years would not be matched with the cost of the machine if the purchase price was subtracted off in the first year, which means that subtracting the cost in one year would not be following the matching principle. By using depreciation, a fraction of the value the machine is subtracted in each year of the assets life which follows the matching principle.

b Calculation of depreciation using the straight line method:

historic cost − residual value/useful life = annual depreciation expense

£30,000 − £9,000/3 = £7,000

c Body Care could have decided on useful life and residual value in the following ways:

- Useful life will depend on how much the asset is used; the more the vehicle is used the lower its useful life will be. The rate at which the asset becomes obsolescent also affects the useful life. Vehicles change shape and offer new features as technology develops, although technology does not change incredibly fast in vehicles. Body Care could look at past experience, the results of other companies' use or take the advice of the vehicle supplier when working out a useful life.
- The residual value of a vehicle will depend on the second hand market for this type of vehicle, which will be affected by the vehicles use; high mileage vehicles will have a lower residual value compared to low mileage ones. Body Care could look at past experience, the results of other companies' use or take the advice of the vehicle supplier when working out the residual value.

3 **a**

	£	£
Sales	95,000 @ 2.50	237,500
cost of sales	111,700	
direct labour (3 × 1,200 × 12)	43,200	
cost of goods sold		154,900
gross profit		82,600
marketing assistant	5,000	
secretary	8,000	
heat and light	1,500	
advertising	8,000	
leasing	20,000	
depreciation	7,000	
total indirect costs		49,500
net profit		33,100
less interest expense		8,000
profit before tax		25,100

Table 10 Profit and loss account for Body Care using FIFO to calculate the cost of sales

b If £40,000 of sales remained unpaid at the end of 1997 then this would still be counted as sales because of the realisation concept. This would mean that profits would be unaffected. However, there would be an extra £40,000 of debtors in the balance sheet which takes debtors to £49,000.

4 **a** Overtrading occurs when a business trades at a level that it is not financially capable of because it has not raised the necessary long term funds to trade at this level. The business can only raise the money to pay for new stock and the extra expenses associated with a higher level of trading by using working capital. This often means increasing the business's bank overdraft. Body Care may face over trading if it accepts the new order from the retail chain. To fund the extra stock it will have to purchase, and pay extra wages, it will need more finance. If this cannot be obtained from long term sources, such as a loan or through shareholders, then Body Care will be forced to increase its overdraft. This will be an expensive source of funds because the interest payments on overdrafts are high. It will also put Body Care in a hazardous liquidity position because it relies on the bank maintaining confidence in its ability to repay the loan. This confidence could be lost because the contract for the extra supply is with a retailer possessing a notorious reputation for late payment.

b Body Care could deal with the problem of late payment by:

- **Offering an incentive to the retailer to pay on time.** This could be in the form of a discount.
- **Charging extra interest to the retailer if it goes beyond the accepted payment period.**
- **Factorising the debt.** This means selling the debt to another company who will collect the debt. The amount paid for the debt by the factorising company will not be the full amount of the debt.

c There are a number of factors that would support the acceptance of the contract from the retail chain. The following factors are monetary advantages to taking the extra order:

- The offer would bring in an extra sales revenue of £150,000. If the company pays on time this could lead to extra cashflow to the business.
- Assuming that direct costs rise in proportion to the increase in revenue, profits would also increase (154,900/95,000 = 1.63).

sales 60,000 @ £2.50	£150,000
direct cost 60,000 @ £1.63	£97,800
	£52,200

- The extra output that needs to be produced could lead to economies of scale that reduce unit costs. Body Care could be able to negotiate a lower price for its input of moisturising cream if it takes the order.

The non monetary advantages to accepting the order would be:

- The new order may well get the Body Care product and brand name more widely known, which could stimulate sales from other sources.
- The increase in turnover could enhance the motivation of the staff who work for Body Care as they see the business gain a prestigious order.

However, there are a number of financial problems associated with accepting the order:

- Overtrading could put severe pressure on the business's cashflow position which could lead to bankruptcy.
- Body Care may not have the capacity to produce the order. It may need to invest in new equipment which would again put it under cashflow pressure.

There are also some key non financial problems with the order:

• Existing customers may not be served as well as the new order takes precedence with Body Care which could mean losing existing customers.
• Body Care may become over reliant on this new major customer which could put it in a vulnerable position if the contract was lost.

The order is a very attractive one to a business that is looking to expand, but it carries risks. Body Care should accept the order if it can minimise the risks. It should secure additional long term finance to cover the threat of overtrading and make sure it maintains its service to its existing customers.

SUNSHINE CREEK MOVES INTO A NEW MARKET

Student book pages 109–110

1 a Reserves are the funds in the balance sheet that are attributable to the shareholders. They can be split up into two types; revenue reserves and capital reserves. Revenue reserves are the accumulated retained profits that a business earns over a period of years. Capital reserves are generated through an increase in the value of fixed assets. For example, if the value of property owned in Sunshine Creek increased then this would be entered upon capital reserves in their balance sheet.
b The value of reserves in Sunshine Creek will rise overtime as it earns more retained profit and or the value of its assets rises. For example, if the value buildings that Sunshine Creek owns increases then the value of capital reserves in its balance sheet will increase.

2 The following items would affect the profit and loss account:

• The cash sales would increase the total sales revenue made in Sunshine Creek's profit and loss account by £10,000.
• The telephone bill would increase Sunshine Creek's indirect costs by £2,000.
• The £4,000 bill paid to the creditor would not affect the profit and loss account because the cost associated with the creditor would have already been included in the profit and loss account.
• The cheques received from the debtor would not affect the profit and loss account because the revenue received from the sale would have already been included in the profit and loss account.

Note: it is assumed that the change in profit does not affect the amount of tax or dividend paid.

sales	+£10,000	£510,000
cost of goods sold		330,000
gross profit		180,000
total overheads	+2,000	92,000
net profit		88,000
interest		24,000
profit before tax		64,000
tax		16,000
profit after tax		48,000
dividends		10,000
retained profit		38,000

Table 11a Revised figures for Sunshine Creek

The following transaction would affect the balance sheet:

• The cash sales would increase the profit of Sunshine Creek by £10,000 which is added to reserves. The £10,000 has been received in cash, so cash increases by £10,000.
• The telephone bill of £2,000 and would reduce profit by £2,000 would reduce the reserves in the balance sheet by £2,000. If we assume the bill is paid in cash, the cash in balance sheet would be reduced by £2,000.

Fixed Assets		£
land		700,000
machinery		85,000
buildings		200,000
		985,000
current assets		
stock		95,000
debtors	−3,000	9,000
cash	+10,000 −2,000 −4,000 +3,000	22,000
		126,000
current liabilities		
trade creditors	−4,000	3,000
overdraft		6,000
tax payable		16,000
		25,000
net current assets		101,000
net assets		1,086,000
owner's capital		
shares		500,000
reserves	+10,000 −2,000	168,000
		668,000
long term liabilities		
mortgage		300,000
other borrowing		118,000
		418,000
capital employed		1,086,000

Table 11b Revised figures for Sunshine Creek

- The bill for £4,000 paid to the creditor would reduce cash by £4,000 and reduce the creditors figure by £4,000.
- The £3,000 received from the debtor would increase cash by £3,000 and reduce debtors by £3,000.

3 Cashflow statement for the opening of the new lodge:

Calculating cash inflows
20 rooms × £40 per room =
£800 revenue per day
7 × 50 = 350 days per year
350 days × £800 revenue per day = £280,000
60% occupancy 0.6 × £280,000
= £168,000 revenue per year

Calculating direct cost
9% of sales revenue 0.09 × £168,000 =
£15,120

Cash inflows	£
sales	168,000
cash outflows	
overheads	15,000
direct costs	15,120
total outflows	30,120
net cash flow	137,880

Table 12 Forecasted cash flow statement for Sunshine Creek's new lodge

4 The financial arguments in favour of opening the new lodge are:

- The annual cash flow forecast which shows that the project will generate £137,880 of cashflow in its first year. Assuming the cashflow remains

constant in future years the project will pay off its initial investment of £190,000 in less than two years. It may well be the case that the occupancy rate rises over time as the lodge becomes established and gains a good reputation.
- The lodge and the vineyard may well complement each other in terms of generating revenue. People who stay at the lodge may well buy wine from the vineyard. This will bring in extra sales and also increase the number of people who know about the vineyard.

In financial terms Sunshine Creek should consider the following disadvantages of opening the lodge:

- The lodge represents a major investment which needs to be financed. If the finance is borrowed it will incur interest costs and if owners capital is used it is less funds for other projects or to be distributed as profits.
- The cashflows are forecasted figures and may not be the actual cashflow the project generates. If the occupancy rates fall below 60% then the project will not yield the cashflows the management expects. However, the occupancy rate could be much higher than expected.

The non financial advantages of the decision are that:

- The lodge will allow Sunshine Creek to spread its risk. If the vineyard has a bad year then the lodge can supplement any shortfall in profits.
- The lodge could allow Sunshine Creek to promote itself more successfully. It will be a place where buyers can be entertained, conferences held and tastings organised.

The non financial disadvantage is that:

- By opening the lodge Sunshine Creek will be moving away from its core business which is producing wine. It has little experience of hotels and this may hinder the success of the project. The lodge could take management time away from managing the vineyard which could adversely affect the vineyard's performance.

There are significant financial benefits from opening the lodge both in the short term and the long term because of the forecasted profits it is likely to generate. There are risks, most importantly the inexperience the current management has in running a hotel, so it may well be worth appointing an experienced manager to run the lodge.

CHEMCLEAN TAKES IN NEW STOCK

Student book pages 110–111

1 ChemClean using FIFO and LIFO to value issues in production:

month	raw material Chemdry	purchased price per litre $	value of purchases $	issued to production	value of issues $	stock
April	200	2.00	400			200 @ $2.00 $400
May				100 @ 2.00	200	100 @ $2.00 $200
July	500	3.00	1,500			100 @ $2.00 $200 500 @ $3.00 $1,500 total $1,700

month	raw material Chemdry	purchased price per litre $	value of purchases $	issued to production	value of issues $	stock
August				300 100 @ 2.00 200 @ 3.00	800	300 @ $3.00 $900
September	800	4.00	3,200			300 @ $3.00 $900 800 @ $4.00 $3,200 total $4,100
October				400 300 @ 3.00 100 @ 4.00	1,300	700 @ $4.00 $2,800
January	900	5.00	4,500			700 @ $4.00 $2,800 900 @ $5.00 $4,500 total $7,300
March				1400 700 @ 4.00 700 @ 5.00	6,300	200 @ $5.00 $1,000

Table 13a ChemClean using FIFO to value issues to production

month	raw material Chemdry	purchased price per litre $	value of purchases $	issued to production	value of issues $	closing stock
April	200	2.00	400			200 @ $2.00 $400
May				100 @ 2.00	200	100 @ $2.00 $200
July	500	3.00	1,500			100 @ $2.00 $200 500 @ $3.00 $1,500 total $1,700
August				300 @ 3.00	900	200 @ $3.00 100 @ $2.00 total $800
September	800	4.00	3,200			200 @ $3.00 100 @ $2.00 800 @ $4.00 total $4,000
October				400 @ 4.00	1,600	200 @ $3.00 100 @ $2.00 400 @ $4.00 total $2,400
January	900	5.00	4,500			900 @ $5.00 200 @ $3.00 100 @ $2.00 400 @ $4.00 total $6,900
March				1400 900 @ 5.00 400 @ 4.00 100 @ 3.00	6,400	100 @ $2.00 100 @ $3.00 total $500

Table 13b ChemClean using LIFO to value issues to production

2 Accountants would prefer LIFO because it is more prudent than using FIFO since it reports a lower profit. This is because the value of stock that is matched with sales is higher using LIFO because the cost of the last stock in rises when prices are rising. LIFO also reports a lower value of closing stock than FIFO which is again more prudent. However, this only applies if the price of stock is rising. If it is falling, FIFO becomes more prudent.

BODDOR UNDERTAKES A PROGRAMME OF COST CUTTING

Student book page 111

1 There are a number of potential sources of finance:

- Boddor's management could try to organise a share issue where external investors are invited to buy shares in the company and put funds into the business.
- Boddor could approach a venture capital company that specialises in providing finance to this type of industry. Venture capital can involve a proportion of the funds in the form of shares and part as a loan.
- The management could approach a bank to organise a loan. This could be a long term loan that is secured against one of the company's assets.
- The company could consider a debenture issue. These are units of debt that are sold to investors. The debenture has a fixed repayment period and pays a rate of interest to the buyer.

2 The possible sources of finance open to Boddor have the following advantages and disadvantages:

- A share issue means raising funds that are a permanent part of the business and do not have to be repaid in the normal course of trading. The dividends that need to be paid to the investors who buy the shares are dependent on the level of profits the company makes each year. If its performance is poor the dividend payment can be reduced. However, issuing shares is not a straight forward business for new companies who do not have a track record that investors can judge in their decision to buy shares. Issuing shares also means reducing or handing over decision making power to the share buyers who will have voting rights at Boddor's AGM. Thus an issue at this stage for Boddor would probably not be possible because of this.
- Venture capital is often made available to small companies like Boddor who are looking for external finance. The shares sold to the venture capitalist have the same advantage as a share issue, although the venture capitalist could ask to take more profits than a normal shareholder. The disadvantage of using venture capital is that Boddor's control over the business could be diluted because the venture capital company wants some influence over the business's decision making.
- A bank loan is probably the most accessible source of finance to the Boddor management. Unlike a share issue, a loan is relatively easy to organise and does not involve dilution of decision making for the existing management. However, unlike a share issue, a loan has to be repaid and interest costs must be paid in full each year whatever the trading performance of the company.
- A debenture issue, like a bank loan, has the advantage of not diluting the existing owners' decision making authority. It may also be possible for Boddor to gain a lower rate of interest

by borrowing directly from the public rather than going through a bank. However, the debentures have to be repaid and they have interest payments. A debenture issue is also more difficult to organise than a bank loan.

3 The bank approached by Boddor for a loan has a responsibility to its own shareholders to make a profit from the loan through the rate of interest it charges, but also to make sure that Boddor has the ability to repay the loan. Once the rate of interest rate has been set for the loan the bank manager would analyse the following factors in deciding whether to offer the loan to Boddor to make sure it is going to be repaid:

- The bank would look carefully at Boddor's cashflow projections. Boddor could be asked to produce a monthly cashflow forecast that shows precisely how Boddor's cash position may change over the trading period. The forecast could highlight points where the company comes under cashflow pressure.
- The bank would look carefully at the asset that the loan is secured against to see whether its value would cover the loan if the loan was not repaid. This would involve valuation of the asset by the bank.
- The bank could look at a detailed business plan where the company sets out who its customer will be, what type of products it will produce, what level of sales and costs it will achieve, what plans for growth it has, how many staff it will employ, etc. This will give the bank some idea of whether the business will be successful or not.
- A business plan would need to be supplemented by forecasted balance sheets and profit and loss accounts for the first few years of trading. Like the plan, they would allow the bank to analyse whether Boddor will be successful or not.
- The bank may also make an assessment of the market and economic environment that Boddor will be trading in. If the trading conditions for the products Boddor is going to mine look favourable then they are more likely to make the loan.

The bank's primary consideration will be Boddor's ability to repay the loan, which is really dependent on how realistic its cashflow projections are, so this would be of primary concern to the bank. In the long term, the bank also needs to be sure that Boddor has the product to be successful over the life of the loan so it will look closely at Boddor's business plan.

UNIT 5
Financial accounting – Section C: Analysing accounts

NELSON FORGES AHEAD

Student book page 121

1 a Explain what you understand by the given ratios:

● The return on **net assets** measured by the equation:

net profit/net assets × 100

The ratio shows the percentage of net profit a company makes on each £1 of assets the company employs. Nelson has a RONA of 22%, which means it makes 22p of net profit on each £1 of net assets employed.

● **Profit margin** is measured by the equation:

net profit/sales × 100

The ratio shows the percentage of net profit the company makes on each £1 of sales. Nelson has a profit margin of 20% which means that it earns 20p profit on each £1 of sales it makes.

● **Asset turnover** is measured by the equation:

sales/net assets

The ratio shows the amount of sales that a company generates from each £1 of net assets it employs. Nelson has an asset turnover of 1.1 which means £1.10 of sales for each £1 of assets employed.

b By taking each ratio in turn it is possible to make an assessment of the relative performance of each company:

● The company that achieves the highest return on nets assets has performed the best under that criteria because it makes more profit from each £1 of assets employed. Nelson with a RONA of 22% has outperformed both Redman and Apex.

● The company that achieves the highest profit margin has performed the best under that criteria because it makes more profit from each £1 of sales it makes. Nelson has achieved a profit margin of 20% which is higher than both Redman and Apex, so it has performed the best under this criteria because it makes more profit on each £1 of sales.

● The company that achieves the highest asset turnover has performed the best under this criteria because it generates more sales from each £1 of assets it employs. Nelson, with asset turnover of 1.1, has achieved the best asset turnover figure because it is higher than both Redman and Apex.

It is clear that when the performance of each company is measured on the basis of RONA, profit margin and asset turnover, Nelson has achieved the best performance.

2 a Return on net assets = operating profit/net assets

$$22\% = \text{operating profit/net assets}$$
$$22\% = £7\text{m/net assets}$$
$$\text{net assets} = \frac{£7\text{m}}{0.22}$$
$$= £32\text{m}$$

b If Nelson's sales increase then it will earn a greater profit, assuming its profit margin stays the same. For each £1 of extra sales it makes it will earn 20p of profit. If sales increased by £1m then profit would rise by £200,000. If the net asset figure remained the same, then Nelson's return on net assets would rise.

3   **a** **Nelson's profit in 1996:**
$$1.25 \times 1995 \text{ profit} = £7m$$
$$£7m/1.25 = £5.6m$$
b A rise in market share means that Nelson's sales will increase as proportion of total market sales. This will give Nelson the following advantages:

- Assuming that total market sales are not falling, a rise in market share will mean that Nelson is increasing its sales. From this it will earn greater profits assuming profit margin remains the same.
- A rise in market share will give Nelson more influence over the road haulage market in the region. The Nelson name will be more widely known which will promote the company.
- A rise in market share will mean that Nelson's sales will increase compared to the other companies in the industry. This will give Nelson more economies of scale than its competitors which will allow it to reduce its unit costs compared to its competitors and allow it to reduce its prices.
- A growing market share shows that Nelson's trading performance has been better than its main rivals. This could enhance Nelson's reputation and allow it to gain access to new long term funds. A share issue is likely to be more successful if potential shareholders can see Nelson outperforming its rivals.

c **Nelson's sales in 1995:**
operating profit/sales × 100 = profit margin

$$5.6m/sales \times 100 = 20\%$$

$$5.6m/0.2 = £28m \text{ sales}$$

4   **a** Nelson, Apex and Redman's efficiency can be measured by analysing how these companies costs have changed as a proportion of sales. The main ratio for this calculation is:

$$\text{cost of goods sold/sales} \times 100$$

This ratio measures a company's overall efficiency. The lower the ratio the more efficient the company's performance will be because the proportion of costs for each £1 of sales will be lower. The efficiency of individual parts of the organisation can be measured by analysing their costs as a portion of sales. For example, the direct labour cost efficiency of Nelson, Apex and Redman can be measured by the equation:

$$\text{direct labour/sales} \times 100$$

The lower this ratio is the more efficiently direct labour is being utilised within the organisation.

  b There are a number of problems associated with using ratio analysis to compare the performances of different organisations. The following problems arise in the comparison of the performances of Nelson, Apex and Redman:

- The ratios being considered for Redman Nelson and Apex are only looked at in one year. This does not allow any trends in performance to be established. Apex's ratios could be improving faster than either Nelson or Redman.
- Only monetary information is considered in ratio analysis. Performance is measured in terms of profits, sales and assets, but non-monetary factors are also important when assessing the performance of organisations. Ratios do not tell us anything directly about the quality of the haulage service being offered by these companies, or the expertise of the people they employ.
- Redman, Nelson and Apex may all be using slightly different accounting techniques in the preparation of their accounts. For example, Redman might

be using straight line depreciation, whereas Nelson and Apex both use declining balance depreciation. This difference may lead to these companies reporting accounts that have not been prepared in exactly the same way, which makes financial statistics more difficult to compare.

- Redman, Nelson and Apex may produce their accounts at different times of the year. This will affect the ratios calculated in accounts because asset values can vary at different times of the year. For example, retailers hold more stocks in the run up to Christmas than they do post Christmas. In the road haulage industry, which is not particularly seasonal, this factor may not be that important, although it could still have an effect.
- The ratios calculated do not take into account changes in the business environment within which Redman, Nelson and Apex operate. Changes in the market and the economy will have a major impact on the ratios calculated. However, these companies do operate in the same local economy and industry, so the impact of these external factors may not affect the comparison of these companies performances as much as other factors.

The major difficulties associated with measuring performances between these companies is probably the fact that only one year's figures are being considered, which severely limits any assessment of performance over time. Non monetary factors that do not show up in the ratios. For example, Redman's performance could have been exceptional if there were management changes taking place in the company.

 c A more meaningful analysis could have been made of Redman, Nelson and Apex by including more information on these companies' performance. This information could come in the form of:

- More ratios could be considered, such as stock turnover, debtors turnover, current ratio, etc. More ratios would build up a fuller picture of these companies' performance.
- Ratios from more years could be considered. This would mean looking at RONA, profit margin and asset turnover for these companies over the last years to establish some trends in performance.
- The results of other companies in the road haulage industry could be looked at. Whilst these might not be in the same region as Redman, Apex and Nelson they could give an idea of how well these companies are performing against other haulage firms in the UK. Redman, Apex and Nelson may be performing very well when compared nationally.
- Economic and market indicators that show the performance of the local and national markets within which Redman, Apex and Nelson operate would be useful to assess their performances given market conditions. If the economy is relatively depressed their performances could be even better that the raw figures suggest.
- It may be useful to have some idea of what Redman, Apex and Nelson aimed to achieve in the current trading period. Have the companies achieved the targets for RONA, asset turnover and profit margin they set out to reach?

The critical information needed to make a more meaningful analysis of Redman, Apex and Nelson is the RONA, profit margin and asset turnover over more years. The current ratios looked at in isolation are limited in terms of assessing where these companies are going without figures over a period of years.

FINANCIAL ACCOUNTING – SECTION C: ANALYSING ACCOUNTS

HARRISON COMPONENTS CONSIDERS MAJOR INVESTMENT

Student book pages 122–124

1 a Harrison's reserves are partly made up of retained profit earned over time. In 1997 Harrison reported a retained profit of £80,000 which would be added to the value of reserves plus any revaluation of fixed assets.

b The rise in depreciation expense in Harrison's profit and loss account could be due to the purchase of new machinery by the company. This machinery would be subject to depreciation and would be added to the existing depreciation in Harrison's profit and loss account.

c When Harrison makes a profit it is liable to pay corporation tax on the profit. The 1997 profit made by Harrison of £380,000 has corporation tax of £160,000 payable on it. However, this is not due to be paid until 12 months after the balance sheet date so it is owed to the tax authorities and is carried as a current liability.

2 a Calculate return on net assets, profit margin and asset turnover for each year.

	1997	1996
return on net assets	440/2,200 × 100 = 20%	360/2,110 × 100 = 17.1%
profit margin	440/5,500 × 100 = 8%	360/5,000 ×100 = 7.2%
asset turnover	5,500/2,200 = 2.5	5,000/2,110 = 2.4

Table 14 Calculations for Harrison Components return on net assets, profit margin and asset turnover

b In each case, the ratios have increased.

- The return on net assets has increased from 17.1% to 20% which means that Harrison is earning more net profit on each £1 of assets employed.
- The profit margin has increased from 7.1% to 8% which means that Harrison is earning a higher percentage of profit on each £1 of sales.
- The asset turnover has improved from 2.4 to 2.5 which means that Harrison is earning a higher percentage of sales on each £1 of assets employed.

The rise in each ratio means that on each of these criteria Harrison's performance has improved.

3 a Liquidity is the ease with which a company can turn its current assets into cash and cover its current liabilities. The most liquid assets Harrison has is cash itself, then debtors and finally stock. In 1997 Harrison had £690,000 of current assets to cover its current liabilities of £490,000.

b There are three ratios that can be considered to assess the liquidity of Harrison:

- **The current ratio:** current assets/current liabilities is one measure of liquidity. This measures Harrison's ability to cover its current liabilities with its current assets. The higher this ratio is the easier it is to cover its current liabilities within its current assets.
- **The acid test ratio:** debtors+cash/current liabilities is a stricter measure of liquidity because stock, which is the least liquid of the current assets, is removed from the ratio. This means measuring the amount of debtors and cash is available to cover current liabilities.
- It is also possible to consider the

amount of cash to cover current liabilities by using the equation: **cash/current liabilities**. This would be the strictest measure of liquidity.

All three ratios should be used to give a full picture of Harrison's liquidity because they provide a measure of liquidity of different degrees of strictness.

c An assessment of Harrison's liquidity.

	1997	1996
current ratio	690,000/490,000 = 1.41	530,000/470,000 = 1.13
acid test ratio	270,000/490,000 = 0.55	230,000/470,000 = 0.49
cash ratio	150,000/490,000 = 0.31	120,000/470,000 = 0.26

Table 15 An assessment of Harrison's liquidity over 1996–97

Each ratio has increased from 1996 to 1997 which means that Harrison's liquidity position has improved. Harrison is in a better position in 1997 to cover its current liabilities with its current assets in 1997 than it was in 1996. The current ratio has increased the most which means that Harrison has increased its stock level faster than its other assets.

4 a There are a number of options for Harrison to raise funds to fund its new machinery:

● Harrison could try to organise a share issue where external investors are invited to buy shares in the company and put funds into the business to purchase the new capital.
● Harrison's management could approach a bank to organise a loan. This could be a long term loan that is secured against one of the company's assets.
● Harrison could use profits generated from their normal course of trading as a source of funds
● Leasing is often used as a way of funding the acquisition of new assets. This is where the asset is rented from a leasing company.

b These are the advantages and disadvantages of each method chosen:

● A share issue is an effective way of raising long term funds. The funds raised do not have to be repaid and the dividends paid to potential investors can be based on Harrison's profits performance. However, issuing new shares does mean diluting the influence of the existing shareholders. A share issue is also a complex way of organising the issue of new funds.
● A bank loan has the advantage of being a relatively straightforward way of raising new funds and organising a loan does not mean diluting the influence of existing shareholders. However, Harrison would have to pay a rate of interest on the loan that is fixed whatever its profits performance and the loan, unlike share capital, has to be repaid.
● Using funds that have been generated internally has the advantage of not having a cost that has to be paid to an outsider or the dilution of the existing shareholders control. However, it does have the cost of a foregone return that could have been earned from an alternative investment. Harrison's could have earned a return with almost no risk by just holding their funds in bank.
● Leasing has the advantage of funding the acquisition of a new asset without Harrison having to raise funds through a share issue. However, the cost of a leasing an asset is much higher than the cost of purchasing the asset.

c Return on net assets is measured using the equation:

$$\text{net profit/net assets} \times 100$$

In the short run, the purchase of new machinery by Harrison would increase the value of net assets owned by the company which would cause the return on net assets to fall. Increasing the value of net assets by £1.4m would give a RONA for 1997 of:

$$440,000/3,600,000 \times 100 = 12.2\%$$

a fall from 20%. In the long term, the new investment by Harrison's would cause the efficiency of the company to rise which would lead to a fall in unit costs and could lead to a rise in net profits. The new investment could also lead to a rise in revenue as the increase in efficiency brought about by the new investment improves the quality of the product and the fall in unit costs allows Harrison's to reduce its selling price.

The impact of the new investment would need to be considered by anyone analysing the performance of Harrison's because in the short run the performance of the company based on RONA would deteriorate initially and then rise in the long term.

NOIR LTD GROW WITH THE SKIING INDUSTRY

Student book pages 124–125

1 Report to the directors of Noir Ltd

The financial performance of Noir Ltd 1996-98

Objective: The aim of this report is to analyse the performance of Noir Ltd using financial ratios based on the following criteria: profitability, liquidity and efficiency.

Report on profitability

The ratios in the table below have been used to report Noir's profitability.

- The return on net assets has increased over the three year period from 35% in 1996 to 100% in 1998 which means that Noir is earning a greater return from each £1 of net assets employed in 1998 than it was in 1996.

- Noir's profit margin has increased from 26% in 1996 to 51% in 1998. This means that Noir is earning a higher net profit on each £1 of sales made in 1998 than it was in 1996.

- Asset turnover has increased from 1.35 in 1996 to 1.95 in 1998. This means that Noir is generating more sales from its assets in 1998 than it was in 1996.

Overall, Noir's performance in terms of profitability has improved a great deal over the period 1996–98. It is achieving a better return on its net assets because it is generating more sales from its net assets and realising a higher profit on each sale made.

£	1996	1997	1998
RONA	900/2,600 × 100 = 35%	1,900/3,350 × 100 = 57%	4,100/4,100 × 100 = 100%
Profit margin	900/3,500 × 100 = 26%	1,900/5,000 × 100 = 38%	4,100/8,000 × 100 = 51%
Asset turnover	3,500/2,600 = 1.35	5,000/3,350 = 1.49	8,000/4,100 = 1.95

Table 16a Report on Noir Ltd's profitability

£	1996	1997	1998
direct cost efficiency	1,200/3,500 × 100 = 34%	1,500/5,000 × 100 = 30%	1,900/8,000 = 23%
indirect cost efficiency	1,400/3,500 × 100 = 40%	1,600/5,000 × 100 = 32%	2,000/8,000 = 25%
Stock turnover	1,200/400 = 3 121 days	1,500/500 = 3 121 days	1,900/700 = 2.71 134 days
Debtors turnover	3,500/300 = 11.7 31 days	5,000/600 = 8.33 44 days	8,000/700 = 11.4 32 days

Table 16b Report on Noir Ltd's efficiency

Report on efficiency

The ratios in the table above have been used to report Noir's efficiency.

- Noir's direct cost efficiency has improved from 34% in 1996 to 23% in 1998. This means that the company's direct costs are falling as a percentage of sales which suggest it is managing its direct costs more efficiently.
- Noir's indirect costs have also fallen as a percentage of sales from 40% in 1996 to 25% in 1998. This suggests that the company is managing its indirect costs more efficiently.
- The stock turnover figure has fallen from 3 in 1996 to 2.71 in 1998. This means that Noir is, on average, taking longer to sell its stock in 1998 than it was in 1996. This suggests that Noir's performance has deteriorated, on the basis that a faster stock turnover is better than a slow one.
- Noir's debtors turnover figure has fallen from 11.7 in 1996 to 11.4 in 1998. This means that Noir's debtors are taking longer on average to pay in 1998 than in 1996. This could be considered to be a deterioration in performance.

Overall, Noir's efficiency in terms managing costs has improved over the period. However, its efficiency in terms of managing stock and debtors could be said to have deteriorated, although the fall in stock and debtors turnover could be due to the rise in sales that the company has experienced.

Report on liquidity

The ratios in the table below have been used to report Noir's liquidity.

- Noir's current ratio has increased from 1.67 in 1996 to 2.5 in 1998. This means that the company has increased the amount of current assets it has to finance each £1 of current liabilities.
- Noir's acid test ratio has increased from 1.17 in 1996 to 1.75 in 1998. This means that the company has increased the amount of debtors and cash it has to finance each £1 of current liabilities.
- Noir's ratio of cash to current liabilities has increased from 0.5 in 1996 to 0.75 in 1998. This means that the company now has more cash to cover each £1 of its current liabilities.
- Noir's gearing ratio has fallen from 38% in 1996 to 30% in 1998. This means that Noir has increased the proportion capital employed that is financed by shareholders funds as opposed to long term liabilities.

Overall, Noir's liquidity in both the long and the short term has improved over the period 1996–98. Its current, acid test and cash ratios have all increased, which means that Noir is better able to cover its short term debts with its current assets. However, Noir has to make sure that it is not tying up assets in an unprofitable manner. In the long term, Noir's gearing has fallen basically because the contribution of Noir's rising profits to reserves. The company's position could be said to have improved because a lower proportion of its capital employed has to be paid for in interest payments.

Conclusion

On the basis of profitability, efficiency and liquidity Noir's performance has improved over the period 1996-98.

£	1996	1997	1998
current ratio	1000/600 = 1.67	1500/700 = 2.14	2,000/800 = 2.5
acid test ratio	600/600 = 1	1,000/700 = 1.43	1,300/800 = 1.63
cash ratio	300/600 = 0.5	400/700 = 0.57	600/800 = 0.75
gearing	1,000/2,600 × 100 = 0.38%	1,250/3,350 × 100 = 0.37%	1,250/4,100 × 100 = 0.30%

Table 16c Report on Noir Ltd's liquidity

2 A further assessment of Noir's performance could have been made by including more information on the company's performance. This information could come in the form of:

- **Ratios from more years** could be considered. This would mean looking at RONA, profit margin and asset turnover for Noir over the last five year to establish a trends over a longer period of time.
- **The results of other companies in the ski manufacturing industry** could be looked at. This information would be vital in establishing how Noir's performance compared to its main rivals. Ratios over a period of years would be useful to compare trends in performance.
- **Economic and market indicators** that show the performance of the local and national markets within which Noir operates, would be useful to assess their performance under given market conditions. If the economy is relatively depressed Noir's performance could be even better than the raw figures suggest.
- It would be useful to **know what Noir had aimed to achieve** over the trading period to assess its performance in the light of its objectives. The company's performance may have vastly exceeded its objectives.

To make a true assessment of Noir's performance it is vital to compare the ratios calculated with those of other firms in the same industry. At present, Noir's performance can only be seen in isolation, so whilst its performance looks impressive, other firms in the skiing industry may have performed even better.

3 There are a number of strengths and weaknesses associated with using ratio analysis to judge the performances of different organisations. Ratios have the following strengths as a way of measuring performance:

- Ratios are objective; they use financial statistics that provide a quantitative guide to a business's performance. Because they are prepared in money terms they can be used to consider a business's performance against other firms. In Noir's case, they have been charted to see how the company's performance has changed over time.
- Ratios, by combining two financial statistics, provide a relative figure that is more useful in assessing a firm's performance than a raw piece of financial data. For example, Noir's net profit figure is not as meaningful as its RONA because the RONA takes into account the size of Noir. Thus this figure can be used to compare businesses and look at changes in performance over time.

However, ratios have the following weaknesses:

- Only monetary information is considered in ratio analysis. Performance is measured in terms of profits, sales and assets, but non monetary factors are also important when assessing the performance of organisations. The ratios considered do not tell us anything directly about the quality of the products produced by the company, or the expertise of the people they employ.
- An important aspect of assessing Noir's performance is making comparisons between its ratios and other firms in the same industry. However, businesses often use different accounting techniques in the preparation of their accounts . Noir might be using straight line depreciation, whereas another firm in the industry is using declining balance depreciation. These differences may lead to these companies reporting accounts that have not been prepared in exactly the same way which makes financial statistics more difficult to compare.

- Another problem of making comparisons between Noir's performance and other firms in the same industry is that companies may produce their accounts at different times of the year. This will affect the ratios calculated in accounts because asset values can vary at different times of the year. In the skiing industry, for example, manufacturers may build up stocks at certain times of the year because of the seasonal nature of the business. As stock levels increase the net asset value rises which would give a low RONA figure. Accounts that are prepared when there is a peak in stock levels will give a lower RONA figure than those prepared when there is a reduced stock figure.
- Ratios do not take into account changes in the business environment within which Noir operates. Changes in the market and the economy will have a major impact on the ratios calculated. Skiing equipment is a relative luxury which means that demand will rise if the economy is experiencing buoyant growth. This would have a positive impact on Noir's performance and would need to be taken into account when assessing it.

Despite their weaknesses, ratios do provide a basis on which an assessment of Noir's trading performance can be measured. However, a full picture of its performance would need to be made in the light of non monetary considerations, such as the quality of its products, and the market environment within which Noir is trading.

UNIT 6

Management accounting – Section A: Budgeting

THE SHOREHAM NURSERY BUDGET

Student book page 141

1 a Budgets are important to Shoreham Nursery for the following reasons:

- Budgets help managers in their task of resource planning. They will tell the managers of Shoreham's the amount of labour, stock and capital that is needed in the coming financial period. For example the levels of sales budgeted will allow the managers at Shoreham to budget for the stock of plants they will need to order.
- Budgets will help the managers at Shoreham set objectives for the coming financial period. The budgeted sales figure for the business can be used to motivate the sales staff at the Nursery.
- Budgets can be used as a method of control within Shoreham. The sales revenue and costs set out in the budgets will allow management to assess the personnel who are responsible for them. For example, the sales manager can be assessed on the sales figures Shoreham's achieves compared to its budgeted sales.
- Budgets can help in the decision making of the organisation. For example, if Shoreham wished to open up a new outlet, the revenue and cost figures budgeted for the new outlet could help management in making the decision.

Budgets are important to Shoreham because they provide a financial guide that can help the business's future performance.

b Shoreham would need to consider the following factors in setting up it budgets:

- The objectives it has set for the organisation. These provide the direction for the budget because this is what the business wants to achieve in the coming financial period. If Shoreham sets itself the objective of achieving a certain return on net assets for the coming finanicial period then it will need to budget for a certain level of sales and cost to achieve the profit to yield this return on net assets.
- In allocating responsibility for the budget, Shoreham would have make sure it appoints the personnel capable of achieving the budget and make it clear to them what they have to achieve. It is important that the personnel are capable of delivering budget and that they are clear in terms of what they have to achieve.
- Shoreham needs to make sure that effective policies and strategies are put into place to achieve the objectives in the budget. For Shoreham this means setting buying, selling and marketing policies and strategies. These could be policies and strategies that Shoreham has used in the past or new ones to use in the future.
- The preparation of forecasts is important because it puts precise figures into the budget. Figures can be set for sales, prices and costs, etc. The forecasts have to be in line with the objectives set and be communicated clearly to the personnel who are responsible for delivering the budget. It is important that each aspect of Shoreham's activities is set out in clear forecasts which are then brought together in the summary budgeted balance sheet and profit and loss accounts.
- Is is important that the budget is

implemented using the policies and strategies set out in the in the budget and that the workforce is motivated to achieve the budget.

- At the end of the financial period the performance of Shoreham needs to be compared to the figures set out in the budget. The review has two purposes: one is to judge the performance of the organisation against its budget, the other is to assess the quality of the budget set.

It is important to see that the whole process of setting up a budget is an integrated one, with each stage of the budgeting process dependent on another. A successful budget is one where each stage is carried out successfully. For example, Shoreham will only achieve its objectives if the policies and strategies set out in the budget allow them to do this.

2 a Sales are important in the budgeting process because the sales figure will influence all the other figures in the budget. This is because sales volume determines the activity levels within Shoreham. Sales determine how much stock the business needs, how many workers will be employed and how much capital will be needed.

b As the sales figures rise in Shoreham's budget, costs rise as well. Cost of sales and labour costs are direct costs, which means they will rise as the activity level of the nursery goes up. If the Nursery sells more plants it will need more stock which increases cost of sales, and as they employ more staff it increases the labour cost. In this case, indirect costs also rise perhaps because more advertising is used and more heat and light is used at higher activity levels.

c Monthly net profit figures.

£						
sales	75,000	80,000	90,000	100,000	120,000	125,000
cost of sales	45,000	48,000	54,000	60,000	72,000	72,000
labour cost	15,000	15,000	17,000	17,000	20,000	20,000
overheads	5,000	5,000	7,000	7,000	8,000	8,000
total cost	65,000	68,000	78,000	84,000	100,000	100,000
net profit	10,000	12,000	12,000	16,000	20,000	25,000

Table 17a Shoreham's monthly net profit figures

d Budgeted profit and loss account.

£		
sales		590,000
direct costs		
cost of sales	351,000	
labour	104,000	
cost of goods sold		455,000
gross profit		135,000
overheads		40,000
net profit		95,000

Table 17b Shoreham's six month budgeted profit and loss account

3 Shoreham will come up against the following problems in trying to set up its budget:

- Budgets are all about the future which is by its very nature uncertain.

The uncertainty associated with external business environment make the setting budgets difficult. For example, the sales actually achieved by an organisation may differ a great deal from the budgeted figure. The market environment may not be as bouyant as Shoreham expected which would lead to a fall in volume and mean that the company has to sell more products at discount prices than it expected. The fall in volume could mean that the amount of stock needed would be lower than the budget and not as many workers would be required as budgeted for. It is clear that a change in one variable in a budget will affect lots of other variables that are dependent upon it.

- Uncertain events can also arise within the organisation that can make setting budgets difficult. Shoreham will not be able to allow for uncertain events, such as the breakdown of an important machine, or an industrial dispute. This type of event could push costs up and mean that the business cannot meet its target sales volume.
- Because certain factors, that are beyond the control of management, can mean that a business does not achieve its budgeted figures, it is difficult to judge the personnel responsible for delivering the budget purely on the actual figures. It would not be fair to assess the sales manager at Shoreham for missing his sales targets if the market was not as bouyant as expected when the budget was set up.
- In order to set up a successful budget, Shoreham must be able to motivate its staff to achieve the targets it has set. If employees fail to work towards the objectives set in the budgets then it will be very difficult for Shoreham to achieve its budget. For example, if department managers exceed their spending targets then the costs set in the budgets will be exceeded by actual costs.

The main problem for Shoreham in setting up its budget is uncertainties associated with the external business environment. Shoreham will have some control over internal events that could affect the budget as well as problems of motivating staff, but it has no control over changes taking place outside the business.

THE JB PROCTOR BUDGET

Student book page 142

1 **a** A flexible budget is a budget that changes as a business achieves different activity levels. When JB Proctor drew up its budget it divided its costs up into fixed and variable costs. The change in activity level was reflected by a change in sales; as sales change variable costs change (or flex) and this is allowed for in the costs in Proctor's flexible budget.

b Fixed budgets are set and the costs and revenues within the budget do not change with activity levels. Because of this fixed budgets are not suitable for measuring business performance. For example, if the direct cost of Proctor is set at £130,000, and its actual costs turn out to be £150,000 then it could be concluded that Proctor's performance was poor in terms of its ability to control its costs. However, this cost figure does not take into account the change in activity level which would naturally make Proctor's direct costs rise. If Proctor sells more conservatories it will need to buy in more raw materials and use more direct labour, which will make its direct costs increase.

BUSINESS STUDIES : A CORE CURRICULUM TEACHER'S BOOK

c Produce a flexible budget for JB Proctor

	£ 50%	£ 100%	£ 150%
sales revenue	100,000	200,000	300,000
variable direct labour cost	20,000	40,000	60,000
variable direct material cost	45,000	90,000	135,000
total direct costs	65,000	130,000	195,000
gross profit	35,000	70,000	105,000
indirect costs	40,000	40,000	40,000
net profit	(5,000)	30,000	65,000

Table 18a A flexible budget for JB Proctor

2 a, c

	£ 150% budget	£ 150% actual	variance
sales revenue	300,000	320,000	20,000(F)
variable direct labour cost	60,000	80,000	20,000(A)
variable direct material cost	135,000	140,000	5,000(A)
total direct costs	195,000	220,000	25,000(A)
gross profit	105,000	100,000	5,000(A)
indirect costs	40,000	42,000	2,000(A)
net profit	65,000	58,000	7,000(A)

Table 18b Profit and loss account for JB Proctor's actual level of activity

b Variance is the difference between a budgeted figure and its actual outcome. For example, Proctor budgeted to achieve a sales revenue of £300,000, but the sales figure actually achieved was £320,000; this gave a variance of £20,000. A favourable variance occurs when the actual figure increases profits compared to the budgeted figure, and it is adverse when the actual figure gives a lower profit compared to the budget. Proctor's direct material cost is an adverse variance because the actual cost is higher than the budgeted figure which reduces profit.

d The actual direct labour could have exceeded the budgeted figure because the wage paid to direct labour could have been higher than that budgeted for. Proctor's direct labour force could have negotiated a higher wage than the company forecasted when setting up its budget.

e Fixed costs include; rent, power, administration, depreciation and marketing costs. Whilst these do not vary directly with activity levels it is possible that they could change over time and be different from the figures forecasted in a budget. For example, Proctors rent could have been increased during the time period of the budget or the company may end up spending more on advertising than it set out in its budget.

A NEW STAND FOR WALTHAM TOWN FC

Student book page 143

1 **a** The intial cost for Waltham Town would be the cost of constructing the stand. This would include building and fitting costs.

b The running costs would include the labour and overheads incurred by Waltham Town over the projected life of the project.

c The following factors would have to be taken into account when setting the revenue projections for Waltham Town.

- Waltham Town will have to forecast how many tickets it will sell in each year of the project. This will be based on the capacity of the stand which is 10,000. The number of tickets sold in the stand each year could be projected by using market research. It could also look at the number of tickets it has sold in previous year, as well as the ticket sales of similar clubs who have built new stands.
- Waltham Towns revenue from ticket sales will be dependent on the number of games the club plays during the season. There will be league, cup and friendly matches that will all generate revenue.
- Waltham Town will need to set a price for the tickets in the stand. There will not be one set price but different prices for different sections within the stand. This would range from the cheapest seats to the cost of executive boxes within the stand. The club will need to work out how many of each price the club will sell.
- Waltham Town will need to consider how much revenue it will generate from other products and services it could generate from the stand. This could be from revenue it gets by franchising food stalls.

d There are a number of problems associated with setting the revenue projections.

- Ticket sales can be very difficult to project. There are the normal problems of projecting sales volume for any problem, but in the case of football this is made more difficult because sales will be affected by the success of the team which is not predictable. If the club is very successful and gets promotion then sales would be much greater than if they stayed in the third division or even fell to the bottom of the league.
- It is difficult to judge what ticket price Waltham Town will be able to set. If ticket sales are intially disappointing then the price of tickets may have to be reduced. Alternatively, if the club is successful tickets could be sold at much higher prices.
- It is difficult to predict how many games Waltham Town might play in a season. League matches can easily be forecast, but the number of cup matches played is much more difficult to predict becasue it depends on the success of the team.

Ultimately, Waltham Town's revenue is difficult to forecast because of the nature of football where revenue is so dependent on the success of the team which is difficult to predict.

2

year	0	1	2	3	4	5
cash inflows £'000'		2,100	2,300	2,400	2,400	2,400
cash outflows £'000'	4,900	200	200	200	200	200
net cashflow £'000'	(4,900)	1,900	2,100	2,200	2,200	2,200

Table 19 Cashflow table for the Waltham Town FC stand project

3 a

Payback

2 years (900/2,200 × 365) 149days

Average annual rate of return

$$\frac{(1{,}900 + 2{,}100 + 2{,}200 + 2{,}200 + 2{,}200 - 4{,}900)/5}{4{,}900} \times 100 = 23.26\%$$

Net present value

year	0	1	2	3	4	5
cash inflows £'000'		2,100	2,300	2,400	2,400	2,400
cash outflows £'000'	4,900	200	200	200	200	200
net cashflow £'000'	(4,900)	1,900	2,100	2,200	2,200	2,200
discount rate	1	0.91	0.83	0.75	0.68	0.62
present value	(4,900)	1,729	1,743	1,650	1,496	1,364

(1,729,000 + 1,743,000 + 1,650,000 + 1,496,000 + 1,364,000) - 4,900,000 = £3,082,000

Table 20 The use of net present value to assess project feasibility

b The new stand yields a positive net present value of £3,082,000. On this basis the project should be accepted because it yields more than the 10% discount rate that could be yielded if the money were put into a bank. The payback of 3 years and 149 days and average annual rate of return of 23.26% cannot be used to make a decision because no target has been set for these two results.

4 A number of other factors would need to be taken into account before Waltham Town can make a decision about whether the project should go ahead or not.

- Targets need to be set for each of the investment appraisal techniques. For example a target for the payback period should be set. If the project meets the targets set then the project should go ahead.
- Waltham Town could compare the returns of this project with other projects they might embark on. This could be a smaller stand or building a leisure centre to be attached to the ground.
- Waltham Town could use the internal rate of return as an additional method of investment appraisal to judge the project.
- It is important for Waltham Town to judge whether the project fits in with the long term strategy of the organisation. If the club is looking to expand in the long term then this new stand would fit into the strategy of the organisation.
- There may be non monetary factors that need to be considered. A new stand may have to be built to comply with relevant health and safety regulations.
- The economic and market environment would need to be looked at carefully. If the economy is about to enter recession then Waltham Town may not want to go ahead with the project.

WARWICK LTD REPLACE THREE VANS

Student book page 144

*This question has been set with Warwick Ltd purchasing 10 rather than 3 vans as set in the original question.

1 The table shows the cashflows, for each alternative, for each year.

Outright purchase	0	1	2	3	4	5	6
cash outflows		110,000					
cash inflows						10,000	
net cashflows		(110,000)				10,000	
Leasing							
Cash outflows		30,000	30,000	30,000	30,000	30,000	
Cash inflows			9,000	9,000	9,000	9,000	9,000
net cashflows		(30,000)	(21,000)	(21,000)	(21,000)	(21,000)	9,000
Hire purchase							
cash outflows	28,600	22,880	22,880	22,880	22,880	22,880	
cash inflows						10,000	
net cashflows	(28,600)	(22,880)	(22,880)	(22,880)	(22,880)	(12,880)	

Table 21a Shows the cashflows, for each alternative, for each year. The cash inflows and outflows for outright purchase, leasing and hire purchase are summarised in each section of the cashflow table

Outright purchase	0	1	2	3	4	5	6
cash outflows		110,000					
cash inflows						10,000	
net cashflows		(110,000)				10,000	
discount rate	1	0.91	0.83	0.75	0.68	0.62	
present value		(100,100)				6,200	
Leasing							
cash outflows		30,000	30,000	30,000	30,000	30,000	
cash inflows			9,000	9,000	9,000	9,000	9,000
net cashflows		(30,000)	(21,000)	(21,000)	(21,000)	(21,000)	9,000
discount rate	1	0.91	0.83	0.75	0.68	0.62	0.57
present value		(27,300)	(17,430)	(15,750)	(14,280)	(13,020)	5,130
Hire purchase							
cash outflows	28,600	22,880	22,880	22,880	22,880	22,880	
cash inflows						10,000	
net cashflows	(28,600)	(22,880)	(22,880)	(22,880)	(22,880)	(12,880)	
discount rate	1	0.91	0.83	0.75	0.68	0.62	0.57
present value	(28,600)	(20,821)	(18,990)	(17,160)	(15,558)	(7,986)	

Table 21b Shows how discounted cashflow can be applied to each option for acquiring the vans. The cashflows generated by each option are multiplied by a 10% discount factor to give their present values

Warwick Ltd: assessment of the purchase of the vans using net cashflow figures. Using the non-discounted cashflows the cheapest method is outright purchase:

Outright purchase: £110,000 − £10,000 = £100,000

Leasing: (£30,000 + £21,000 + £21,000 + £21,000 + £21,000) − £9,000 = £105,000

Hire purchase: £143,000 − £10,000 = £133,000

Warwick Ltd: assessment of the purchase of the vans using discounted cashflow. Using discounted cashflows the cheapest method of acquiring the vehicles is leasing:

Outright purchase: £100,100 − £6,200 = £93,900

Leasing: (£27,300 + £17,430 + £15,750 + £14,280 + £13,020) − £5,130 = £82,650

Hire purchase: £28,600 + £20,821 + £18,990 + £17,160 + £15,558 + £7,986 = £109,115

BEDWYN LTD CHOOSE A PROJECT

Student book page 145

1

Should Bedwyn Ltd choose to expand into Europe or concentrate on expansion in the UK market?

Objectives

- To analyse the returns of each project using average annual rate of return, payback, internal rate of return and net present value.
- To consider the influence of the economic environment, the Bedwyn's market experience and the human aspect of the decision.

Investment appraisal

- **Average annual rate of return:** Project A yields the highest ARR which means that the average percentage return on the initial outlay is higher for project A than B. A return of 15.2% compared to Bs 10% means that for each £1 invested in project A the annual return is 15p, but only 10p for project B.
- **Payback:** Project B generates cashflow that pays back it initial investment in two years whereas B takes five years. On this criteria, expansion in the UK market seems to be the safer option compared to expansion into Europe.
- **Net present value:** Expansion into Europe yields a higher NPV than expansion in the UK, so on this criteria A has the best performance. NPV discounts the future cashflows of each project which means that it takes into account the time value of money.
- **The internal rate of return:** This method of investment appraisal gives the project a discount rate that yields an NPV of zero. Project B has a higher IRR than project A which means it performs better performance than project A. Project B yields a better return for each £1 invested when the cashflows are discounted.

On the basis of total return from the project, expansion into Europe appears to be a better prospect than expansion in the existing UK market. However, project B yields its returns more quickly and earns a superior rate of return on each £1 invested when the project is discounted. One reason for this is that expansion into Europe ▶▶

earns it greatest returns in years six, seven and eight which are subject to the greatest rate discounting, whereas the UK project earns its greatest return in the its first and second years when the discount rate is lower.

Non monetary factors

- The economic environment: the European market probably holds the potential to increase revenue by more than the UK market because of the potential number of consumers. However, Bedwyn will have to deal with the problems of changes in the exchange rate which will affect the price they sell their products at in Europe. Whilst concentration on the UK market means that Bedwyn does not reach the same number of consumers, it does not come up against the problems caused by changes in the exchange rate.
- Europe is a new market that has yet to be exploited by Bedwyn. The company has been successful in the UK with the product so it may well be able to transfer this success into Europe. However, the European market poses the following problems to Bedwyn: there will be differences in language, technical differences in the standards of fire equipment and additional transport costs. By opting for the UK market, Bedwyn will not be exposed to the same difficulties. However, the company will be expanding into the mass market in the UK when it has only had experience of the industrialised sector.
- Project A will mean changing production techniques which the workforce are unhappy about. Any successful project will need to have the support for the workforce to make it successful so project B would look more favourable. However, Bedwyn cannot let a major opportunity be affected too much by the views of the workforce because workers are often reluctant to accept change. The size of the European market will mean a signifcant increase in employment opportunities.

Conclusions

- Project A will yield significantly higher cash flows than project B, although B pays back more quickly and earns a higher internal rate of return. On this basis, expansion in the UK is less risky than expansion into Europe, but it does not give the same potential for expansion.
- Expansion into Europe carries greater risks than expansion in the UK because Bedwyn will face the challenge of the exchange rate, language differences, transport costs and problems with the workforce.

Recommendation

Despite the risks involved, Bedwyn should expand into Europe if it wants to grow as a company and become more profitable in the future.

UNIT 6

Management accounting – Section B: Costing

NINKA LTD'S TWO COST CENTRES

Student book page 157

1 a Direct costs are those costs that can be directly associated with the production of the product or service produced by an organisation. For example, Ninka has incurred direct labour and material costs in the production of its printers. Direct labour would be the wages paid to workers who work on the production line producing the computers, and direct materials would be the components used to make the computers.

b A cost centre is an area within a business that has costs associated with it operation. Within Ninka the departments that produce the ink jet and laser printers are costs centres that have direct and indirect costs allocated to them.

c Depreciation is the fall in the value of fixed assets over time. When Ninka buys its machinery it will fall in value due to wear and tear and obsolescence. This fall in value needs to be accounted for in the preparation of Ninka's accounts. The annual depreciation expense represents a proportion of the cost of the asset that needs to be taken away from Ninka's profit and the accumulated depreciation of the asset needs to be subtracted from the assets value in the balance sheet.

2 a Overheads are the indirect costs of Ninka's operations. Energy costs, maintenance, rent, management salaries and marketing costs.
b Monthly overhead expense: £4.8m/12 = £400,000
c Monthly overhead expense: £400,000 × 0.4 = £160,000
d The high proportion of depreciation expense as part of Ninka's costs can be explained by the following factors:

- Ninka could be a capital intensive company that has a high proportion of capital costs as a share of its total cost.
- The capital that Ninka owns may fall in value very quickly because it is technically advanced and becomes obsolete very quickly.

3 a Absorption costing is the allocation of overhead to a cost centre. This is done by sharing out the overhead on the basis of direct costs. Ninka has chosen to allocate overhead on the basis of direct materials. Absorption costing has to be used because overheads cannot be specifically identified with a cost centre because they tend to be applied to the whole business. For example, both the ink jet and laser printer cost centres are in the same factory so the rent cost is applied to both centres and cannot be identified with a specific centre.

b, c

£		ink jet	laser
direct labour	105,000	45,000	60,000
direct materials	1,210,000	250,000	960,000
total	1,315,000	295,000	1,020,000
overhead cost	4,800,000	250/1,210 × 4,800,000 = 991,736	960/1,210 × 4,800,000 = 3,808,265
total cost	6,115,000	1,286,736	4,828,265
units produced		10,000	12,000
cost per unit		128.67	402.35

Table 22 Overhead and unit cost calculations for Ninka Ltd

4 Low unit costs can be used as a measure of efficiency because it represents the money value of resources used to produce a single unit of output. The lower the cost per unit the more efficiently resources have been used to produce a single unit. However, this figure would be misleading when it is used to compare different products, as in the case of the ink jet and laser printers:

● The materials used to produce the laser and ink jet printers will have different costs. The materials used to produce the laser printers are likely to be more expensive than those used to produce the ink jet printers, which will lead to a higher unit cost.

● The labour used to produce the laser printers could have a higher cost than that used by the ink jet cost centre. This could be because the workers needed to produce the laser printers are paid a higher wage. It may also take longer to produce a laser printer, because it is a more complicated product to produce than an ink jet printer, which means the wage cost of each laser printer is higher than the ink jet printer.

● The higher direct material cost of the laser print department means that it will be allocated more overheads. This means the laser department uses more expensive materials and in turn it will be allocated more overheads, which is something the manager of the laser department will have no control over.

5 a Ninka's accountant would want to look at depreciation separately for the following reasons:

● Depreciation is a the cost associated with the fall in the value of capital equipment over time. The capital that produces each printer could be used exclusively by each department which means the depreciation expense of each department can be identified specifically.

● The depreciation expense is such a large proportion of total overhead it should be allocated separately and not on the basis of direct materials. This is because direct materials is not a good basis on which to allocate depreciation.

b The best way to allocate depreciation for each department would be to use the actual deprecation expense of each machine used by either the ink jet or laser printer department. If this is not possible a relevant way to allocate the depreciation expense would be by the value of machinery in each department.

6 a

£		ink jet	laser
total cost	6,115,000	1,286,736	4,828,265
units produced		10,000	12,000
cost per unit		128.67 × 1.2	402.35 × 1.2
mark up		20%	20%
selling price		£154.40	£482.82

Table 23 Calculation of the selling prices of Ninka Ltd's two printers

b There are a number of other factors that Ninka would want to take into account when setting the price of its ink jet and laser printers:

● The price the consumer is willing to pay is important. Consumers may be willing to pay a higher price than the prices based on the 20% mark up, or they may not be willing to pay a price as high as those with a 20% mark up. Market research would be important to Ninka in working out how much Ninka believes their potential consumers are willing to pay.

- The price charged by other firms in the market is important in the pricing decision for the printers. If Ninka charges a price above their main competitors then they may well not achieve the sales that they need.
- The price charged will be influenced by Ninka's overall marketing strategy. The company may wish to achieve a high sales volume with their computers which means they would reduce their price to try and maximise sales. On the other hand, Ninka might want to achieve a higher profit margin on a lower sales volume.
- The price that Ninka charges for other products that it sells will be an influence on the pricing decision. Ninka may be producing other products, like personal computers. If they set a lower price for their PCs, they might try to make more profits on the package by setting a higher price on printers.

In any pricing decision made by an organisation it is important to take into account cost factors and marketing factors when making the final decision.

OLYMPIC SPORTS SHOE LTD WISHES TO RAISE SALES

Student book page 158

1 a Absorption costing is the allocation of overhead to a cost centre. This is done by sharing out the overhead on the basis of direct costs. Olympic Sports has chosen to allocate overhead on the basis of direct labour. Absorption costing has to be used because overheads cannot be specifically identified with a cost centre because they tend to be applied to the whole business. For example, the squash pro, tennis elite and badminton squad products are cost centres in the same factory, so the heat and light expense is applied to all the centres and cannot be identified with a specific centre.

b, c

£	total cost	squash pro	tennis elite	badminton squad
direct labour	72,000	35,000	22,000	15,000
direct material	123,000	52,000	46,000	25,000
overhead	45,000	35/72 × 45,000 = 21,875	22/72 × 45,000 = 13,750	15/72 × 45,000 = 9,375
total cost		108,875	81,750	49,375
units produced		6,000	5,000	3,000
unit cost		18.15	16.35	16.46
mark-up 32%		18.15 × 1.32	16.35 × 1.32	16.45 × 1.32
selling price		23.96	21.58	21.73

Table 24 The overhead allocation and price for each Olympic Sports product

2 a Absorption costing can be carried out in a more precise way. To do this Olympic Sports would have to go through the following steps:

- The overhead would need to be divided up into different types. Olympic Sports would have indirect labour, management salaries, depreciation, marketing expenses, etc. as different types of overhead.
- Each type of overhead would then be allocated to a cost centre on basis that was relevant to the centre. For

example, the depreciation expense could be allocated on the basis of the value of capital in the cost centres, or administration could be allocated on the basis of the number of employees in each cost centre.

- Once the basis for allocation has been chosen each type of overhead needs to be apportioned to a cost centre. For example, if administration costs were £10,000 and the tennis elite cost centre had 25% of the employees then it would be allocated 25% of the administration overhead.

By using this more advanced method of absorption costing Olympic sports is able to allocate overheads on a more scientific basis than just lumping all the overhead together and allocating it.

b The main problems associated with this more advanced method of absorption costing are:

- Choosing the basis on which to allocate the overhead. Rent can be allocated on the basis of floor space occupied by each cost centre and depreciation can be allocated by the value of machinery, but how can management salaries be allocated? Is it possible to work out the amount of time a manager at Olympic Sports works with a cost centre if they have responsibility for the whole business. Marketing, selling and distribution costs are also very difficult to apportion to an individual cost centre.

- Once the basis has been chosen it is questionable how accurate it is in terms of allocating overhead. For example, just because the squash pro cost centre has more direct labour than the other cost centres it does not necessarily mean that it will account for more administration.

- This method of absorption costing is more complex and time consuming than simple full costing.

Overall, it can be argued that the time and effort put into producing a more accurate method of apportioning overhead is not really worth it because absorption costing can never really be accurate. However, more accurate absorption costing does mean that large individual units of overhead cannot necessarily distort the costing for each cost centre. Depreciation could be a major item of overhead that needs to have a large apportionment to one cost centre if it has a machine with very high depreciation expense. This will not come out in a full costing statement where all the overhead has been lumped together.

3 **a**

Tennis Elite mark-up	£ unit cost × mark-up	£ price	demand	£ revenue
20%	1.2 × 16.35	19.62	6,000	117,720
25%	1.25 × 16.35	20.44	5,800	118,552
30%	1.30 × 16.35	21.26	5,600	119,056
32%	1.32 × 16.35	21.58	5,000	107,900

Table 25 Olympic Sports Ltd's revenue on four different levels of mark-up price

b On the basis of the figures provided, Olympic Sports should choose the 30% mark-up because it yields the highest revenue. However, the figure for the 32 % mark-up are misleading because they are based on the actual amount produced and not the forecasted sales. It is likely that the price increase from £21.26 to £21.58 would not have caused sales to fall by quite as much, given the forecasts for the other prices. That said, even if sales only fall to 5,500 (given the relationship between mark-up and sales volume) it would only yield a revenue of £118,690.

c There are a number of different strategies that Olympic Sports could use as they try to change the price of the tennis shoes. It is important to remember that the company will be selling to retailers who will then be selling the shoes on to the final consumer. Thus the price charged by Olympic Sports will have an influence over the final selling price of the product but the retailer will also have an influence.

- The price of the shoes could be heavily discounted to achieve a high level of sales volume. This would give Olympic Sports a high market share and allow the name of the company to be spread throughout the market. The high sales volume would also allow Olympic Sports to buy materials in greater quantities which could give the company lower costs. However, the evidence from the market research suggests that if Olympic Sports went for a low, 20% mark-up it would lead to a lower revenue and, assuming unit costs remain the same, profit. Using a lower price could conflict with the marketing objectives of the business which could be to give the Olympic Sports brand a quality image. A price that is below the level of the business's main competitors may mean that the product develops a cheap image in the eyes of the consumer.
- Olympic Sports could choose the strategy of choosing a high mark-up and setting a premium price for their tennis shoes. The forecasted revenues show that this price would yield a higher revenue than the lower price and, assuming unit costs stay the same, a higher profit. The premium price may also give the product a quality image in the mind of the consumer which could strengthen the brand. However, a high price which leads to lower volumes could mean that Olympic Sports misses out on possible economies of scale that may be derived from higher sales volumes. Retailers may also be reluctant to buy a product that is only going to sell slowly when they as retailers could be looking for a high turnover from the product.
- Olympic Sports could follow a strategy of selling their tennis elite shoe at a similar price to their main competitors. From a marketing perspective, this allows the tennis elite to have a similar perceived image in the mind of the consumer as its main competitors, which, assuming the competitors have a strong brand image, could enhance the image of the tennis elite shoe. By setting their price at the same level as their competitors, Olympic Sports will avoid a possible price war where competitors reduce their own prices to match a lower price charged by Olympic Sports. The disadvantage of this option is that consumers will not be able to use price to distinguish Olympic Sports tennis shoes from their competitors on the basis of price. The aim of the marketing director of Olympic Sports is to try and raise the sales of the tennis elite shoes which is unlikely to happen if prices are pitched at the same level as the product's competitors. The competitor's prices may also be at a level that means the tennis elite yields a low revenue and profit.

If the aim of Olympic Sports is to increase the sale of its tennis elite shoes then a lower price seems to be the most relevant option. However, the company must make sure that this price is supported by the other elements of its marketing such as advertising and distribution.

FINANCIAL DATA FROM THE MINI OHMS COMPANY

Student book page 159

1 a Fixed costs are those costs that do not change with output. Examples of the fixed costs that Mini Ohms has are: rent, capital depreciation, and management salaries. Variable costs are those costs that change with output. As a company produces more these costs increase. Since Mini Ohms produces more electric motors it will use more raw materials and these costs will rise.

b Operating profit calculation:

		£		£
sales	£25 @ 10,000	250,000	£25 @ 30,000	750,000
variable cost	162,500		487,500	
fixed cost	150,000		150,000	
total cost		312,500		637,500
Profit		(62,500)		112,500

Table 26 The calculation of operating profit for Mini Ohms at 10,000 units

c Profit/sales revenue × 100

112,500/ 750,000 = 15%

2 a

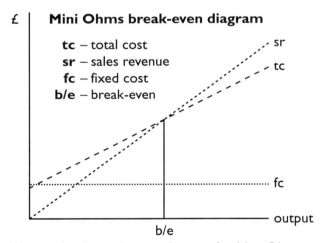

Figure 4 A break-even diagram for Mini Ohms

b Break-even calculation

$$\frac{\text{fixed cost}}{\text{price} - \text{unit variable cost}} = \text{break-even point}$$

unit variable cost calculated as
0.65 × 25 = 16.25
£150,000/£25 − £16.25 = 17,143 units

3 a The lowest price for a special order is based on the marginal cost of the unit produced. The marginal cost is the unit variable cost which is £16.25 and this is the base point for any discount price. Any price in excess of £16.25 would make a positive contribution and would be acceptable. For example, a price of £16.30 would give a contribution of: 6,000 × (£16.30-£16.25) = £300.

b The project would be beneficial for the following reasons:

● Mini ohms should accept the order if the price they can get makes a positive contribution. The larger this contribution is, the more attractive the offer is to Mini Ohms. If they could get a price of £20 the offer would be worth: 6,000 × (£20 - £16.25) = £22,500.
● This type of contract would also be useful if Mini Ohms is looking to attract a new major contract that they can look to for future sales. This may be important if the buyer pays quickly and this creates good cashflow for Mini Ohms.
● The buyer might also wish to purchase other products from Mini Ohms which could provide greater sales and profits for the company.
● If the new buyer is impressed with products provided by Mini Ohms then

they could recommend Mini Ohms to other companies and generate even more business.
- The extra 6,000 units of output could give Mini Ohms economies of scale which reduces their unit costs and increases profits.

However, there may be problems with the contract.

- If Mini Ohms is operating at capacity and is able to sell all its produces at the normal price, then there would be little point in accepting a offer which they have to discount. Mini Ohms may not have the capacity to produce an extra 6,000 units.
- Setting a discounted price may upset existing customers who normally pay the full price. The existing customers could ask for discount themselves or they might look for another supplier.
- Producing an extra 6,000 units beyond 30,000 units may cause variable costs to rise if Mini Ohms has to pay overtime rates of pay to workers.

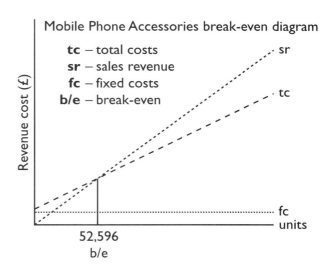

Figure 5 A break-even diagram for Mobile Phone Accessories

In the short term, the offer could be very important if it produces necessary cashflow. But the long term implications are possibly more critical. If Mini Ohms upsets its existing business it may not be wise to accept the offer but if it can be used to generate new business it may be worth it.

A NEW SPEAKER FROM MOBILE PHONE ACCESSORIES

Student book page 160

1 a Mobile Phone could have established the fixed costs associated with the project in the following ways:

- Rent would be a fairly certain cost because Mobile Phone know which factory unit they are going to use and the rent would have been set by a landlord.
- Capital costs could be forecasted by working out the depreciation expense on fixed assets. The annual depreciation is calculated by dividing the purchase price of the asset by its estimated useful life.
- Heat and light could be estimated by using previous figures from the existing factory, along with any estimates provided by the factory owner.
- Marketing expenses could be forecasted from past experience. They may well be set by Mobile Phone according to marketing budget allocated to this particular project.
- Administration and management salaries will be forecasted on the basis of the amount of management and administration time the new factory will take up.

b There are a number of ways that Mobile Phone could forecast demand for the new product:

- Market research using personal interviews from potential consumers in the target market will give Mobile Phone an idea of the consumer's reaction to the product and whether they are likely to buy it.

- Secondary data regarding how many mobile phone users there are would give Mobile Phone an idea of the potential market.
- The price Mobile Phone sets will influence potential demand. If the price is relatively low then the demand is likely to be greater compared to a high price.
- Economic conditions will influence demand. If the economy is relatively buoyant then demand will be high.
- If there is already a lot of existing competition then this will limit demand compared to a situation where there is limited competition.

2 a

	£	
unit labour cost		1.30
unit material cost		1.20
unit variable cost		2.50
unit fixed cost	60,900/200,000 =	0.31
unit total cost		**2.81**

Table 27 Calculation of the unit cost of production if Mobile Phone Accessories achieves capacity

b Selling price is calculated as 30% mark up on fixed costs.

$$1.3 \times £2.81 = £3.65$$

	£	£
sales revenue	200,000 @ £3.65	730,000
variable cost	200,000 @ £2.50	500,000
fixed cost		60,900
total cost		560,900
profit		169,100

c Break-even output

$$\frac{\text{fixed cost}}{\text{selling price - unit variable cost}}$$

$$\frac{£60,900}{£3.65 - £2.50} = 52,956 \text{ units}$$

d Margin of safety

target sales − break-even sales = margin of safety

$$150,000 - 52,956 = 97,044$$

3 The profit that could be earned by importing the product from the Korean manufacturer is set out below.

		£
sales revenue	200,000 @ £3.65	730,000
variable costs	200,000 @ £1.40	280,000
fixed costs		26,000
total cost		306,000
profit		**424,000**

Table 28a Profit earned by Mobile Phone from Korean imports

compared to an existing target profit of:

		£
sales revenue	200,000 @ £3.65	730,000
variable costs	200,000 @ £1.40	500,000
fixed costs		60,900
total cost		560,900
profit		**169,100**

Table 28b Mobile Phone's existing target profit

New break-even:

26,000/(3.65-1.40) = 1.556 units compared to an existing break-even of: 52,956

From these figures the Korean option looks very favourable with a big increase in profits and a fall in break-even sales. However these figures are based on the assumption that the £100,000 transport cost can be allocated to each unit at 50p. It may be the case that for carriages of less than 200,000 units the cost per unit of transport rises as economies of scale are lost. It is also assumed that the price charged remains the same as if the product were produced in the UK. It may be possible to reduce the price of the product and increase sales beyond the target of 200,000.

The non numerical arguments for the switch to Korean production are:

- The reduced fixed costs of production, because a new production unit does not have to be opened, means that the risks associated with the project are reduced. If the product does not sell well then the Korean contract can be terminated without losses. In the UK, machinery would have to be sold off, possibly at a loss.

- The Korean manufacturer may also be a specialist in this type of component. The final product could be of a higher quality than that produced by Mobile Phone.

There are, however, disadvantages to switching production to Korea:

- The components produced in Korea may be of an inferior quality which could damage Mobile Phone's reputation. It could also lead to Mobile Phone missing its target sales figure because consumers do not like the product.
- Once the production of the good is sub-contracted to a supplier, Mobile Phone will lose control over the production and delivery of the product. If the supplier goes bankrupt or is simply inefficient then supply could be interrupted and sales lost.
- Bringing in components from abroad has its own particular difficulties. Corporate cultures differ between UK and Asian companies and Mobile Phone may not find it particularly easy to work with these differences. The sheer distance between the supplier and Mobile Phone presents difficulties of communication.
- Importing products also means contending with the exchange rate. Because changes in the exchange rate alter the final price of buying the product it increases the risks of dealing with Korea. A fall in the value of the Pound against the Korean currency would mean that the components would rise in price. Although a rise in the value of the Pound would mean that the components became cheaper. Overall, the exchange rate does make budgeting for the project more difficult and this is a disadvantage.
- The use of the Korean producer will limit the size of manufacturing in the UK. This could reduce the economies of scale Mobile Phone achieves in other areas. It may also be a threat to other areas of production for the company which could unsettle the existing workforce and reduce their motivation.

There is no doubt that the financial benefits of sub-contracting the components to South Korea would increase profits, assuming the quality, supply conditions, and exchange rate were favourable. However, in the long term Mobile Phone needs to decide on the direction it is going to move in. If it decides to sub-contract production overseas the whole nature of its operation will change from being a manufacturer to being a wholesaler. Does the company really want to move in this direction?

UNIT 7 Human resource management

BLUE CIRCLE CEMENT CHANGING ITS WORKING PRACTICES

Student book pages 179–180

1 a F.W. Taylor put forward the theory of scientific management. His theory centred on the view that workers were essentially lazy and unmotivated and that they were primarily motivated by money. He believed that organisations should, through work study, break down all the tasks involved with a job and provide monetary incentives to workers to carry out these tasks as efficiently as possible. At Blue Circle this would mean taking a part of the cement production process, working out the most efficient way of carrying out this process, and then setting up a bonus scheme for workers who achieve the set level of efficiency in producing the cement. The targets set to the workers would be based on achieving a certain number of units in a given time period, a process called piece work. If the efficiency targets were not met there would be some form of penalty for not achieving them.

b Taylor's view could be perhaps be illustrated by the attitude of the workforce before the changes took place within the organisation. Up until the 1980s, workers received overtime payments for working unsocial hours which often occurred when machinery broke down. Thus there was a financial incentive for allowing machinery to break down. It seems that this was exactly what the workers at Blue Circle were doing: allowing machinery to break down so they could earn more money from the overtime this generated. Taylor would argue that this showed workers acting in their own financial self-interest ahead of the interests of the organisation. It could also be said that increasing basic wage levels for workers to smooth the introduction of new working practices reflected the idea that workers are motivated by money.

c The new payment system introduced by Blue Circle involved increasing basic wage levels, reducing the amount of overtime that workers could work, but introducing flexi-hours as a system of overtime, and the removal of bonuses. These changes will have the following benefits in terms of motivation:

- The higher basic salary offered to the workforce will improve the morale of workers because Blue Circle has improved what Hertzberg would have called maintenance or hygiene factors. Maslow would have illustrated this as the satisfaction of what he called the lower order needs of acceptance, security and physiology. Up until the time when this new pay system was introduced, the wage structure at Blue Circle seemed to act very much as a demotivating factor. With a higher basic salary workers will feel more secure financially and will be able to concentrate on doing a more effective job.
- Under the old payment system, with workers heavily dependent on overtime to make up their wages, workers had an incentive to work inefficiently as opposed to efficiently. The new system of basic pay with no overtime gave workers the incentive to work efficiently.
- The new payment system fits in well with the whole plan for changing

working practices. The simplified payment system will fit in well with the ideas of team working and skills training which puts more emphasis on collective working towards a common aim.

However, a higher basic salary could adversely affect motivation:

- A high basic salary means that workers will receive the same wage no matter how hard they work. This could lead to complacency as workers become accustomed to the higher wages. This complacency could then lead to a fall in motivation.

Overall, the new system has removed a major problem for Blue Circle which is a payment system that leads towards demotivation as opposed to motivation. However, it is important that the level of pay that is set at rate that motivates and then does not allow for complacency.

2 **a** These are the view of the following management theorists:

- Abraham Maslow was an American psychologist who did a considerable amount of work on human needs. His theory of the existence of a hierarchy of needs had a major influence over management theory on motivation. The hierarchy is made up of physical, safety, social, esteem and self actualisation needs. Maslow believed that each need had to been fulfilled completely before the next level in the hierarchy could be achieved. For an organisation like Blue Circle, it is important to realise that to motivate their workforce successfully they must be aware of each stage in the hierarchy needs and how this affects motivation.
- Douglas Mcgregor was an American psychologist who believed that managers could be divided into two types; Theory X and Theory Y. Theory X managers believed that workers were primarily motivated by money, needed to be closely supervised, and respected clear decisive direction from managers. Theory Y managers believe that workers were motivated by the intrinsic satisfaction in their job, could be trusted to work effectively on their own and were willing to contribute positively to decision making.
- Elton Mayo was founder of the human relations movement. He carried out the Hawthorne Studies which looked at the effect changes in working conditions had on a group of female workers. This involved changes in the length of the working day, breaks, lighting and refreshments. After the experiments were finished the productivity of the workers continued to rise and it was concluded that it was not the changes in conditions that affected the worker's motivation but the fact that the workers felt the there was some interest in them. It was concluded that group dynamics and good working relations within groups that are critical to motivation.
- Frederick Hertzberg is also a follower of the human resources approach. He worked on development of Maslow's ideas by developing the two factor theory of motivation. He believed that maintenance, or hygiene factors, such as salary and job security, would, if they were not satisfied, act as demotivators. Motivators of satisfiers are factors that can act as motivators and lead to satisfaction if they were achieved. Motivators include; achievement, recognition and promotion.

b The changes that have taken at Blue Circle could have increased staff motivation in the following ways:

- The introduction of skills training for all workers will improve motivation as the workforce gains greater fulfilment at work. The training will mean that workers will be able to attain the higher order needs identified by Maslow, such as self esteem which is attained through growth in the job. The skills acquired could lead workers to gain promotion which is an important motivator in Hertzberg's theory. Douglas Mcgregor's Theory Y suggests that a workforce with greater skills is also likely to gain greater intrinsic satisfaction from their work and be more motivated as a result.

- The introduction of team working would have been identified by Mayo as critical in raising motivation within the company because he identified the importance of group dynamics in motivating workers. The Hawthorne Studies showed that through team working groups of workers will interact to motivate each other in the workplace. The group or team, will gain identity and importance which will improve motivation. Team working also enhances the feeling of belonging and affiliation which was identified in Maslow's hierarchy of needs. The absence of affiliation prevents workers reaching the highest levels within the hierarchy. Team working towards a common goal introduces achievement in the workplace which is something that Hertzberg identified as a motivator.
- The payment system which raises the basic pay of employees is seen as important by Hertzberg because it deals with an important hygiene factor. If an employee perceives their salary as unsatisfactory then it acts as a demotivator. Maslow looks at the importance of the salary to people in terms of the way it satisfies physiological, security and esteem needs. This shows how an increase in salary will allow workers to achieve higher order needs at work and be better motivated as result of this.
- The fact that the new proposals were drawn up in consultation with the workforce would be viewed as important by management theorists. Consultation would seen as recognition of the workforce which is one of Hertzberg's motivating factors. Mcgregor's Theory Y managers believed that involving the workforce in the decision making process is critical when motivating workers.

It can be clearly seen that the introduction of the new working practices by Blue Circle have followed many of the ideas put forward by the management theorists. The fact that productivity has increased by 300% suggests that the changes made have been successful in motivating staff.

c There would be a number of difficulties in implementing the plan:

- **Cost:** skills training, redesigning jobs and increasing pay will all add to Blue Circle's costs. If costs increase, unless there is a rise in productivity or revenue profits will then fall. Any fall in profits may meet with resistance from the company's shareholders.
- **Change:** there will always be some human resistance to change. Some workers and managers will feel threatened by the changes that have taken place and will try to resist them.
- **Logistics:** a big change like Blue Circle's will mean reorganising the whole organisation. This will take time, lead to mistakes and perhaps cause an initial fall in efficiency. This might unsettle some customers who could feel that their supply might be interrupted.

All these problems needed to be overcome for the change in working practices at Blue Circle to be successful. Thus the planning process needed to be extensive with plenty of consultation and agreement from the workforce. Blue Circle would have needed to have strong leadership to make sure the change was carried through fully.

3 Staff motivation is absolutely critical to Blue Circle's successful performance. Improving staff motivation can have the following benefits for Blue Circle:

- If staff are better motivated then they will work more effectively and their productivity will rise. This is borne out in the evidence from Blue Circle where productivity improved by 300% as a result of the changes in working practices that were designed to raise staff motivation. As productivity improves, Blue Circle's unit costs of production will fall and profits will rise. However, it has to be assumed that improved motivation can lead to a rise in productivity. In some circumstances improved motivation might not necessarily lead to a rise in productivity if it is not possible to increase productivity in a particular job. In service jobs, such as marketing, it would be much more difficult to see an increase productivity.

- Better motivation increases the morale of employees who will be happier and more fulfilled at work. This will lead to a reduction in staff absenteeism and sickness which reduces Blue Circle's costs and increases profits.
- Better motivated staff may produce better quality products as a result of being better motivated. There are less likely to be mistakes in production and the quality of the final products produced by Blue Circle may well rise. If the company produces a better quality of product or service then it may well sell more, increasing revenue and profits. In the long term, organisations that have a higher level of motivation amongst their staff may well enhance the reputation and corporate image of the company, increasing the business's long term profitability and growth.
- A more motivated labour force with improved skill levels will be more flexible. The workforce will be better able to respond to change, such as the threat of increased competition or the onset of recession. If the workforce at Blue Circle can do this then they will be able to protect their sales and market share. A flexible, skilled workforce may be able to bring about positive change within the organisation itself, such as the introduction new production techniques, which in turn improves the organisation's performance in terms of lower costs and higher revenues.

It is clear that staff motivation has a critical impact on an organisation's performance both in the short term in the form of higher productivity, and in the long term in the form of better corporate image. However, performance has been looked at in terms of costs revenues and profits. It is also possible to look at Blue Circle's performance in terms of its success in creating a positive working environment for the staff themselves.

GREAT MILLS – APPOINTING AND TRAINING NEW MANAGERS

Student book pages 180–182

1 The personnel department at Great Mills will have the following basic functions:

- **Recruitment:** the personnel department will be responsible for recruiting employees to work at Great Mills. This will involve the process of analysing the jobs that need to be done by the recruited staff, advertising for staff then interviewing and appointing people.
- **Induction:** once employees have been recruited Great Mills will have carry out an induction programme. This involves introducing a new employee to the business and that the employee understands the objectives, workings and rules of the organisation so that they can carry out their function effectively. The process normally involves staff training,

although the amount and content of the training will depend on the experience of the staff and the demands of the job they will do.

- **Appraisal:** the personnel department at Great Mills will be responsible for overseeing the appraisal of staff performance. This normally involves a series of interviews and observations of staff working to see what their strengths and weaknesses are. Workers will then be rewarded for good performance or guided on how they can deal with any problems.
- **Training:** the training of new and existing staff is an important function of the personnel department at Great Mills. The department will run on-the-job training as well off-the-job course and conferences.
- **Departure of employees:** the personnel department is responsible for overseeing the departure of employees from the business. Employees will leave Great Mills when they retire, resign, are made redundant or they are dismissed. The legal aspects of this area of the department's work are critical. For example there are legal procedures that have to be adhered to by the personnel department when an employee is being dismissed.
- **Physical and social welfare of employees:** the personnel department at Great Mills will be responsible for looking after employees by making sure their conditions at work meet the standards set by the Health and Safety at Work Act. The department will also be responsible for counselling workers when they have problems at work and dealing with disputes between workers and managers.
- **Industrial relations:** in many firms it is the responsibility of the personnel department to look after maintaining the relationship between workers and employees. This could be important when there are wage negotiations, redundancies and industrial disputes.

2

a Great Mills could advertise for management trainees in a variety of locations including: newspapers, trade magazines, posters in their stores, the internet, careers fairs, employment agencies, Great Mills company publications and on the radio. Posters within their stores could be an effective low cost method of advertising for trainee managers which would be effective because they target people who are, because they are in the store, interested in DIY products and the Great Mills stores. However, this is not a place where people would necessarily look for a job so it would need to be supported by a campaign in a national newspaper targeting a broad job-seeking audience. However, this would be expensive and does not necessarily reach people who are interested in DIY.

b The key features of an advert for a trainee manager for Great Mills would be:

- An eye catching headline that initially draws people to the advert.
- A job description which sets out what is required of a Great Mills manager.
- A statement of what qualifications, skills, and characteristics are required from Great Mills managers.
- Details of what benefits managers at Great Mills can expect to receive, such as pay, holidays, pensions and bonuses.
- There need to be specific details on how people can apply.

c The location of a job advertisement is important because a business wants to make sure that it targets as many good potential candidates as possible within a given budget for the advert. The type of employee Great Mills wants have to be exposed to their job advert. Store management is a skilled, demanding job that will need ambitious, motivated applicants. Thus the type of newspaper that is chosen for an advert would have to be read by this type of person. Great Mills wants to find people who are interested in DIY so any magazine that attracts this type of readership would target the right people.

The contents of the advert are important because they have to catch the attention of the target candidates and then persuade them to apply for the job. The wording of the advert should allow target candidates to identify themselves with the job of a trainee manager. If people want responsibility and interest in a job then this needs to be made clear in the advert. It is important that good potential candidates are not put off by the wording of the advert.

If the wording and placement of the advert is poor then it will not attract the quality of candidates that Great Mills requires. This means that the whole selection process will be adversely affected and time will be wasted due to lack of the right quality of candidate. In the end, the quality of managers appointed will not be as good as it could have been.

3 **a** The three additional questions that could be asked would be:

- How would you make the people you are managing do what you want them to?

This question is designed to see what type of manager the candidate is and how they would relate to the employees they are managing. This is absolutely critical in a management job where so much of a manager's time running a DIY store would be spent getting the workforce to work in the way the manager wants. Answers to the question like 'leading by example' would perhaps be the type of answer Great Mills would want.

- What is the most important thing that motivates you to do a good job?

The success of the store will depend a great deal on the motivation of the staff and their leadership comes from the motivation of the manager. If the manager is someone who is motivated by the desire to do the best work possible, then this type of candidate might be looked at ahead of one that said they were motivated by having power over people.

- How would you deal with a customer who was complaining?

Another major aspect of managing a business is dealing with customers. Customers are at their most difficult when they are complaining and dealing with them is real skill. Answers to this question, would give the interviewer an indication of the candidate's skills in dealing with a customer. A candidate whose answer suggested they were prepared to listen and deal with the complaint themselves to keep a satisfied customer would perhaps be selected ahead of someone who said they would get a sales assistant to deal with problem.

b Personal interviews are useful in that they allow the personnel department at Great Mills to assess through a series of questions what the strengths and weaknesses of a candidate are. The interview can do this on a number of different levels:

- The content of a candidate's response will tell the interviewer about a candidate's intelligence, assertiveness, use of language, and whether the candidates views match up with the requirements of a store manager at Great Mills.
- The manner in which the candidate responds to the questions will give the interviewer an idea of the candidate's personality. For example, if a candidate becomes overly flustered by an interview, how well will they react to the pressures of running a major retail outlet? If the candidate is aggressive and does not listen well then questions could be asked about their ability to deal with staff and customers.
- The candidate's body language in an interview will give the interviewer an idea about the candidate's personality. If the candidate's body language is open and relaxed then they might have

the confidence necessary to be a good manager.

- Interviews can be conducted with a group of interviewees together. In this situation, the interviewer will be able to see how the candidate reacts to other people, which would give the interviewer an idea of the candidate's ability to work within a team.
- Interviews are very important in assessing a candidate's communication skills which are important in store management. These skills will come across in the content and manner of the candidate's answers, as well as through their body language.

However, interviews can only offer Great Mills a snapshot of the candidate's strengths and weaknesses. It is possible through interview training and preparation for candidates to push forward an image of themselves that is not truly reflective of their real personality. Interviews on their own could mean that unsuitable candidates are appointed which leads to poor managers and a higher staff turnover. Thus it is important that interviews are supported by other methods of assessing candidates, such as isometric tests.

4   a The interview with the a member of Great Mill's store staff would be useful because:

- The candidates may let down their guard when talking to someone who they feel is not officially part of the selection process, despite the fact that they are. The candidate may give away more to the store staff about the real motives behind their application and what really motivates them in a job.
- The manner in which the candidate deals with the member of the store staff is important because it will give Great Mills an idea of how well the candidate might relate to people who will be their subordinates. The ability of the candidate to relate well is absolutely vital for a potential store manager.

   b This is a group exercise that could be used in Great Mills management process.

- The candidates would be broken down into groups of four or five.
- Each group will be given a DIY management issue to deal with.
- The issues would be: launching a new product into the store, dealing with a complaining customer, dealing with a member of the store staff who has discipline problems, and increasing the sales of store that has seen a fall in turnover.
- The candidates would be given a 15 minute time limit to come up with a plan of how to deal with each issue.
- Each group would have to give a five minute preparation of their plan.

This exercise would try to assess the candidates skills in the following ways.

- **Team work:** by working groups it will be possible to assess how the candidates will work as a team.
- **Leadership:** the interaction of candidates within the group will allow Great Mills to judge the leadership skills of the candidates.
- **Problem solving:** the way in which individual candidates contribute to the formation of a plan will illustrate their problem solving skills.
- **Communication:** the contribution of individual candidates within the group exercise as well as the final presentation will demonstrate the candidate's communication skills.
- **Motivation:** the determination to produce a good presentation will illustrate the candidate's motivation.
- **Perception:** the way the candidates worked with other in their group as well as their common sense and eye for detail would come across through work on the exercise.
- **Processing:** in the exercise it would be possible to see how the candidates processed information, picking out relevant points and seeing their importance in the context of a solution.

5 A successful recruitment and training programme will have the following benefits for Great Mills.

● Effective management is vital in the successful operation of a store. Generally speaking a store will only run as well as the quality of its manager. A good manager will create high morale amongst the staff, run the shop efficiently and attract lots of satisfied customers. If this happens then the revenue earned by the store will rise and its costs will fall, which in turn increases profits.

● If recruitment and selection is not successful then staff turnover amongst managers will rise. Managers will be unhappy and will under-perform which could lead to resignation and redundancy. If manager turnover is very high then the stores will not be managed effectively because of the constant change in leadership.

● Successful managers that come from effective recruitment and selection, will provide the supply of the new senior managers within the Great Mills organisation. If this supply is plentiful then this will contribute to the long term success of the company.

UNIT 8 *Operations management*

MARKS & SPENCER DECIDE ON STORE LOCATION

Student book page 206

1 a Here are two other factors, apart from those in the case study that Marks & Spencer might take into account:

- **The availability of a skilled workforce.** Marks & Spencer expect the highest standards from their employees. The availability of people who can meet their standards could influence their location decision. However, shop work does not require very specialist staff, such as the specialist software designers that a computer company might need, which means that most locations would be able to provide the staff they need. So whilst the availability of skilled staff would be a factor it would not be as important as some others.

- **Government influence** would be another factor that Marks & Spencer would need to consider; particularly local government. Planning laws can have a major impact on a store's location because local government may not allow the development of a department store. Marks & Spencer's planning department will know where local authorities are sympathetic to planning applications and where they are not and this will influence any development decision.

Other factors that could be discussed would be: the number and type of other outlets near the location and proximity of suppliers.

b There are a number of factors that will determine the cost of developing a particular site:

- **The cost of purchasing the land** is a major factor. The land cost will depend on demand and supply factors. If the land is limited in supply, as is the case in a city centre, then it will be expensive. If there is high demand for a site, as is the case in certain city centres where there is a large number of potential customers then again the cost of the site will be high. The same principles would apply if the site was rented.

- There will be **legal expenses** associated with development of Marks & Spencer stores. These will vary depending on how much time needs to be spent gaining planning permission from a local authority to open a store.

- Once a site has been acquired by Marks & Spencer there is **the cost of construction and fitting the store**. The cost of labour and materials will be relatively similar across the country although there could be slight regional differences. In south east England the cost of labour may well be higher than the north. The structure and position of a building will affect its development costs. An out of town site, with easy access for contractors and new regularly designed buildings will be cheaper than city centre sites, with their difficult access and older, more irregular buildings.

c The potential revenue a Marks & Spencer store could generate will depend on:

- The number of potential customers that a store can attract. In retailing, the stores location is vital. A city centre site will give the store access to a large number of potential customers, although certain city centres will be busier than others. In some towns the number of potential customers is falling as people move to out of town sites to do their shopping. Also, some locations in city centres will be better than others. For example, locations outside the main shopping area in the business district, which is dominated by offices, will attract relatively few shoppers. Out of town sites can attract large numbers of potential customers and revenue. For Marks & Spencer, a large number of similar stores located on a site will attract large numbers of shoppers and revenue.

- The disposable income of customers determines how much customers will spend once they are in the store. The relative affluence of customers will vary from area to area. Prosperous areas of south east England, where disposable incomes are high may well generate more revenue for a Marks & Spencer store than areas in the north of England. However, whilst incomes may be lower in the north, people may have more money to spend in retailers because other costs, such as housing and transport, are not as high.
- Location could influence the type of products a store sells. Out of town sites, where access for customers is easier may attract more people who want to buy furniture, whereas city centre sites attract more food shoppers. The impact on revenue depends on the volumes sold, but it could affect the overall total.

2 The advantages and disadvantages of Marks & Spencer moving to an out of town site are:

- The development costs for the store are likely to be lower because land is cheaper and building and fitting stores is easier than city centre sites. However, out of town sites do need to be developed from scratch in many cases which means planning and construction costs. City centre sites can be developed more quickly if they are already built.
- The nation's shopping habits are changing with people now doing their shopping out of town using their cars. People find it easier to buy major household items out of town because they find it easier to get their purchases home in the car. There are parking restrictions in town centres that makes this more difficult. However, Marks & Spencer do sell a wide range of clothing and food products that are still attractive to city centre buyers.
- Because of motorway access, people from a much wider catchment area can be drawn to Marks & Spencer stores. City centres, with awkward access, cannot do this in the same way. However, out of town sites do limit shoppers to car owners or people with access to cars. City centres have public transport facilities for people who do not have cars.
- Store locations can be used to enhance the Marks & Spencer brand. The wide variety of store locations both in city centres and out of town makes sure that people see the stores and experience them. If they were moved out of city centres then customer experience would happen less often and the Marks & Spencer brand may well be weakened. Certain city centre stores offer prestige locations that cannot be obtained from out of town sites. This particularly applies to Central London. Tourists are also more likely to be attracted to city centre sites in locations such as Bath, York, and Cambridge.

Whilst there obvious cost and revenue advantages to moving to out of town sites, it is still important for the name of Marks & Spencer to be on show in city centres.

ALLIED BAKERIES BREAD PRODUCTION

Student book pages 207–208

1 **a** There are three types of production:

- **Job production** takes place when a product is produced as a single, one-off unit of output. In this method, once the completed product has been finished, the next unit of output is begun. Job production applies to large products, such as bridges, and roads, but it also applies to smaller units, such as made to measure suits. The company that supplies Allied Bakeries with its specialist ovens uses job production.
- **Batch production** takes place where a number of units of the product go as a batch through different stages in the production process. At each stage of the system, the whole batch is processed before it passes onto the next stage. Small bakeries may produce on a batch basis. For example, 10 units of specialist birthday cakes pass through a mixing stage, to a baking stage, then to an icing before they are eventually completed. Once this batch has been completed the next batch of cakes can be started.
- **Flow production** occurs when individual products move from one stage of production to the next as soon as they have completed the previous stage in production. Products move continuously through each stage, without any breaks in production to allow another unit or batch to be started. Flow production is used to produce large quantities of standardised products.

b Allied Bakeries produces Sunblest white bread using flow production because each standardised unit passes continuously through each stage of production.

c Flow production is used by Allied Bakeries because the demand for the bread they produce is high and constant. A continuous flow of production where each stage of production can be carried out by capital set up to allow a continuous flow of the product. Flow production means that a consistent standard of bread can be produced and this standard can be easily checked at different stages in the process. Because machinery can be set up in a formation to allow a continuous flow, labour costs are minimised. Thus flow production means that mass produced bread is the consistent standard that customers expect, and it is produced much more efficiently than job or batch production which would not be practical and would increase unit costs considerably.

d Bread produced in small quantities for specialist market segments could be produced using batch production, but it is hard to see when job production would be used for economically viable output. Batch production by a small bakery may well take place when it is producing, for example, crusty loaves. A batch of crusty loaves will be started and completed before a new batch of a different type of bread is started. Whilst Allied bakeries produces different types of bread, such as Allinsons and Sunblest, they would not be produced in batches. Demand for these loaves it too high and they can be produced much more efficiently using flow techniques.

2 **a** Production efficiency is the level of output achieved from each unit of input in the production process. Output, in the case of Allied Bakeries, is a unit or loaf of bread. Inputs are the labour, capital and materials used by the company. The more loaves of bread produced from a given quantity of inputs, the more productively efficient the company is. Many companies just use labour as their input to make their efficiency measure simple. If bread output produced by workers at Allied Bakeries rises from 1,000 loaves per worker to 2,000 loaves per worker, then we would say that production efficiency has increased.

b Output of loaves per worker employed by Allied Bakeries would be one way of measuring the company's efficiency. However, this method excludes capital as an input. Because bread production at Allied is so capital intensive, capital must be taken into account. Allied could use the unit cost of producing a loaf of bread as a measure of productive efficiency. In a given period:

Total cost/units produced = unit cost

will give a money measure of efficiency. The lower the cost per unit of each loaf produced, the more efficient production has been.

c Lean production is a range of measures used to reduce waste and improve productive efficiency. The measures that can be used are:

● **Minimising the time taken in product development**, by reducing the time lag between the initial product idea and getting the product onto the market. Allied Bakeries would need to minimise the time between the idea of a new type of wholemeal loaf and the product being sold to customers.
● **Just-in-time stock management** is introduced to reduce stock holding costs. This would be important for Allied in terms of its stocks of flour and other ingredients.
● Kaizen working practices can be used, where group working is introduced to improve motivation. Allied Bakeries would arrange teams of workers being made responsible for each area of the production line.

d Just-in-time is a stock management system where the amount of stock held is based on current demand. The sales department at Allied Bakeries initiate the stock purchasing process through the orders they receive from their customers. If Allied Bakeries receive orders from different supermarket chains, then they will send an order for the finished bread to the production department, who in turn will send an order to the buying department for stocks of ingredients. The buying department will then order only enough ingredients from Allied's suppliers to meet the level of demand specified. This means that ordering and production take place 'just-in-time' to meet the customer's order with stock being held in small quantities for a minimum amount of time. This would reduce stock holding costs for Allied, which includes the cost of wasted ingredients that deteriorate if they are held in stock for too long. It also makes the workforce have to work at 100% capacity. If motivation levels fall below this in any part of the production process then there will be delays in production.

3 a Quality control is the process of checking the quality of work bought in or completed by an organisation. Many large companies employ a quality control team to check quality against specific criteria set by the organisation. However, more progressive organisations use employees at each stage of production to check the quality of their own work. The quality control team at Allied Bakeries would be concerned with checking quality of bread at each stage of the production process. This process ensures that the final product Allied produces is a high enough standard to fully satisfy the consumer.

b There are a number of stages in the production process that Allied Bakeries need to implement quality control:

● In the mixing part of production quality control will involve looking at

the standard of the ingredients being used. The proportions of the different ingredients being used would also need to be monitored. Once the dough has been mixed it would need to be checked for its consistency, perhaps by looking at its water content and weight.
- In the baking stage the heat of the ovens would need to be checked, along with the heat of the bread. As bread rises in the baking process its size and weight could be measured.
- In the cooling process temperature must again be checked. It may not be possible to bag bread that is too hot. After cooling, the bread may have changed size and weight, so it again should be weighed and measured.
- Once cut, the thickness of slices should be measured. The taste of the bread could also be checked at this point.
- Once bagged the packaged bread can be monitored to ensure that the way it looks will appeal to consumers.
- The customer complaints department, as well as the feedback received by the sales staff, will test the reaction of consumers to the quality of the final product.

The overall quality of the bread produced by Allied Bakeries will depend on the success of quality control at each stage of the production process. If careful quality control takes place from the start of production then quality problems further down the line are less likely to occur. For example, if the wrong quantities of ingredients are used, then this will affect the weight, size and taste of the bread.

 c Allied Bakeries could employ total quality management as a strategy to improve the quality of the bread that it produces. This would involve changes in the way the company ensures quality in its final product. TQM is a philosophy of quality control that allocates the responsibility of quality control to all workers and managers throughout the organisation. All the workers and managers at Allied Bakeries would be responsible for checking the quality of the bread produced by the company. This removes the need for a quality control department because their function is carried by those producing the product. As Allied's workforce will become more responsible for guaranteeing the quality of their own output, they are more likely to improve the quality of what they produce.

To introduce the TQM Allied Bakeries could use the following strategy:

- Initial discussion regarding the introduction of TQM should take place at senior management level, where specific objectives for the application of TQM should be set. Extensive research should be carried out, and representations from experts in the use of TQM should be heard by management.
- Once the decision has been taken to implement this process it needs to be communicated with the workforce at Allied. All employees need to be fully aware of the objectives of the changes taking place and how they will be affected. At this point feedback should be invited, which may generate useful ideas and allow the workforce to feel they are involved in the decision making process.
- The workforce would need to be reorganised to make the introduction of TQM effective. Workers could be organised into teams and allocated specific responsibilities. Personnel changes would have to take place to make certain that effective leaders are in place to ensure the process is managed effectively.
- Before the system of TQM can be started, extensive training of employees needs to take place. Everyone has to know what their job is in terms of achieving quality so that they are able to carry out their tasks effectively.

- Once TQM is introduced, it has to be carefully monitored to see whether it has improved quality. This can be done through reports on quality being reviewed by senior managers. Also, final feedback from customers through customer complaints rates should be carefully observed.

The success of TQM depends on the motivation of the workforce. It is vital that the company takes steps to make sure that morale is maintained at a high level. This could come through improvements in pay and conditions, and clear recognition by senior management of the importance of the workforce's role in making TQM work.

ACD VIDEO LTD ORGANISE A MAJOR CONTRACT

Student book pages 208–209

1
a The project for ACD Video is set out in the network diagram Figure 6.
b The earliest start times for each task in ACD's project are set out in Table 29, column 3.
c The latest finish times for each task in ACD's project are set out in Table 29, column 4.
d Critical path for ACD's project: A–D–G–J–K–L
e The total float for each activity in ACD's project is set out in Table 29, column 5.
f A five week delay in the delivery of the camera components would take activity C to 11 weeks, which would increase the project's completion time to 51 weeks. Remember, there is a £1,000 per week penalty clause in the contract for each week the project goes over 50 weeks. The total penalty is £1,000.

2
a The cheapest method of a reduction of weeks would be:
A – 2 weeks × 5,000 = £10,000
D – 1 week × 2,000 = £2,000
K – 1 week × 8,000 = £8,000
L – 1 week × 8,000 = £8,000
Total cost = £28,000
b With the time reductions put into place, activities A D G K L remain critical. However, A C F I K L also becomes a new critical path.

Activity	Duration	Earliest start time	Latest finish time	Total float	Free float
A	9	0	9	0	0
B	5	0	12	7	0
C	6	9	16	1	0
D	5	9	14	0	0
E	3	5	15	7	0
F	10	15	26	1	0
G	9	14	23	0	0
H	8	8	23	7	7
I	7	25	33	1	1
J	10	23	33	0	0
K	6	33	39	0	0
L	8	39	47	0	0

Table 29

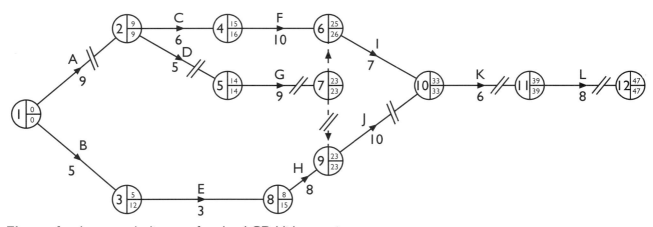

Figure 6 A network diagram for the ACD Video project

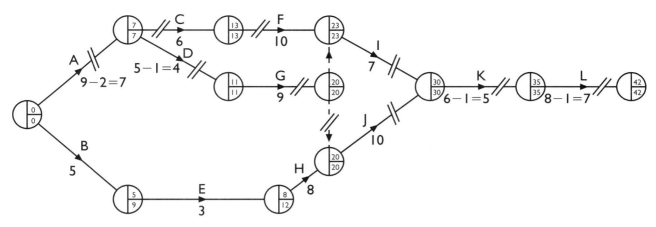

Figure 7

3 **a** Stock holding costs represent the cost to an organisation of holding stock for a given time period. These costs include insurance, depreciation of the stock, storage costs, the cost of labour needed to manage and check the stock, and the interest costs of money tied up in stock for long periods of time. For example, ACD Video may incur considerable insurance costs whilst holding such valuable equipment.

Stock out costs represent the costs incurred by an organisation when it runs out of stock. In the short term, this will be the loss of a sale if a customer needs to go somewhere else for a product. If the stock, as in ACD Ltd's case, is needed to complete a particular job, then it will be the cost in terms of not completing the job on time. ACD will be forced to pay penalty costs if it runs out of stock and the project is delayed. In the long term, stock out costs can be considerable because customers, having found an alternative source of supply, go permanently to another supplier.

b The optimum stock level is where the stock holding costs are equal to the stock out costs as shown in the diagram below. For ACD Video to establish its optimum stock level it needs to find out how its stock costs change as it holds different quantities of stock. For example, the cost of insurance and the cost of lost interest incurred if cash is tied up in stock both increase when more stock is held. ACD needs to establish the rate at which these costs change as they hold more stock. Stockout costs in ACD's case can be assessed in terms of the financial penalties built into its contracts, as well as its loss of reputation if jobs are not completed on time. When ACD has balanced off the extra holding costs of stock against stockout costs then this would be the optimum stock level.

c ACD would face a number of problems in trying to establish an optimum stock level. Stock holding costs do not necessarily follow the smooth pattern indicated by the graph.

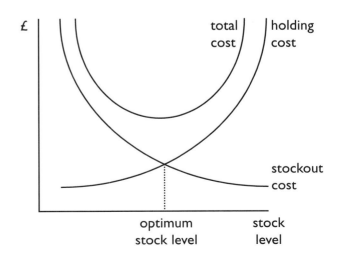

Figure 8 Diagram to show ACD's optimum stock level

The insurance cost may well increase in steps as the value of the stock held increases. Stockout costs can be very difficult to forecast. For example, the penalty costs incurred by ACD are predictable, but the loss of reputation resulting from a delayed contract is not. A further contract with another company may or may not be cancelled if their present contract is delayed.

d ACD may well have a problem holding stock because of the nature of the product it produces. The systems it designs are tailored specifically for the customers needs, which means that the equipment needed for one job may not be needed for another job. This means that stock held for one job may not necessarily be of use for another job. ACD would have to carry a large of stock of components which could be used for a whole variety of jobs and this would mean large holding costs. This could be made worse in market where developments in new technology could make stock held for a long period of time obsolete. However, it could be argued that camera housings and accessories are likely to be pretty standard, and could be used for most jobs, even if the more technical equipment could not.

BADEN AND CLARKE DEVELOP A NEW PRODUCTION SITE

Student book pages 210–211

1 a Just-in-time is a stock management system where the amount of stock held is based on current demand. The sales department initiate the stock purchasing process through the orders they receive from their customers. If Baden and Clarke receive an order for an alarm system, then an order for the finished good will be sent to the production department, who in turn will send an order to the buying department for sub-assemblies and components. The buying department will then order only enough components and sub-assemblies from Baden and Clarke's suppliers to meet that particular order. This means that ordering and production take place 'just-in-time' to meet the customer's order, with stock being held in small quantities for a minimum amount of time.

b The advantages of just-in-time are:

● Just-in-time means that stocks are reduced to very low levels which reduces stock holding costs. For Baden and Clarke this would mean that the costs of stock depreciation, management and insurance are all reduced.

● It means that cash does not have to be tied up in large quantities of stock. The liquidity of the company is improved and it has money to put into other, more profitable areas, such as investment in new machinery.

● Baden and Clarke will reduce the cost of wasted stock that is held, but is not used and becomes obsolete.

● Because the organisation has to respond so quickly and efficiently to consumer demand in the JIT system the whole organisation becomes leaner and more efficient. If a department at Baden and Clarke know that any over run in their production time will delay the whole production process then they are more likely to work efficiently.

In the short run, the improvement in liquidity and reduced stock holding costs will be a significant advantage to Baden and Clarke, but in the long run the improvements in efficiency may prove to be the biggest advantage to the company.

c Applying JIT has the following problems:

- Baden and Clarke need to have very reliable suppliers who deliver on time and without any lead time. If they do not, then JIT will not work, and there will always be a delay in production.
- The workforce have to work at 100% capacity. If motivation levels fall below this in any part of the production process then there will be delays in production. It is vital that industrial relations are good and that the whole workforce of Baden and Clarke are behind the proposal. If there are any industrial relations problems then the JIT will not work.
- Demand does not always follow a predictable pattern. If Baden and Clarke does not have any back up production to cover surges in demand then the company will not be able to satisfy all its customers and will suffer stockout costs.

JIT has significant risks attached to it. If the system does not work then there will be significant stockout costs for Baden and Clarke and they may well lose customers. Its success relies on its suppliers and workforce all combining effectively to meet the demands of the system.

2 a Total Quality Management (TQM) is a philosophy of quality control that is the responsibility of all workers and managers throughout the organisation. All the workers and managers at Baden and Clarke would be responsible for checking the quality of the products produced by the organisation. This removes the need for a quality control department because their function is carried by those producing the product. TQM, along with quality circles and JIT production, are all part of Kaizen, the Japanese management technique used to improve the quality of the organisation as a whole.

b There are a number of advantages to Baden and Clarke of using TQM:

- The quality of the alarms produced by Baden and Clarke will improve which will reduce the cost of rejected and wasted products.
- The cost of employing a quality control department will be removed.
- Baden and Clarke's workforce will become more responsible for guaranteeing the quality of their own output and their own motivation could improve as a result of this.
- If the quality of the final product produced by Baden and Clarke goes up then customer satisfaction will improve, making customers more loyal and attracting new customers.

In the short term the fall in waste costs will be a significant advantage to Baden. In the long term, the improvement in the quality of the alarms they produce will enhance the size and loyalty of their customer base.

c Baden and Clarke will face a number of problems when they are trying to implement TQM. These problems are:

- The whole system of TQM revolves around the workforce taking responsibility for quality control. The workers given this responsibility at Baden and Clarke may not have the level of training and intelligence to carry out the specialised tasks they are required to do. However, workers can be trained. Workers who produce a product will also have specific knowledge on where defects and problems occur in the production of their own output.
- There will be training costs for workers in quality control. However, Baden and Clarke will benefit in the long run from a more highly trained labour force, not just in quality control but in other aspects of production.
- There may well be transition problems in moving to TQM because it is a different corporate culture to Baden and Clarke's existing culture. Workers may well find it difficult to

work under a new system where they are supposed to check the quality of products for themselves. The workforce may be reluctant to reject work they have produced themselves, or they may be lazy when it comes to checking work. A quality control department would not have these difficulties. However, any major change would have the same type of difficulties. If the change is carefully managed the transition difficulties could be minimised.

Whilst there are significant short term transition problems in moving to TQM, the long run advantages in terms of producing better products and development of customer base may well outweigh them for Baden and Clarke.

3 a Figure 9 shows the network diagram for Baden and Clarke's project.
b The earliest start times for Baden and Clarke's project are set out in Table 30, column 3.
c The latest finish times for Baden and Clarke's project are set out in Table 30, column 4.

Activity	Duration	Earliest start time	Latest finish time	Total float	Free float
A	2	0	4	2	0
B	3	0	7	4	2
C	16	0	16	0	0
D	3	2	7	2	0
E	5	5	12	2	0
F	2	10	14	2	0
G	2	12	16	2	2
H	3	12	19	4	4
I	3	16	19	0	0
J	2	19	21	0	0
K	5	21	26	0	0

Table 30

d Critical path for Baden and Clarke's project is C–I–J–K
e The total floats for Baden and Clarke's project are set out in Table 30, column 5.

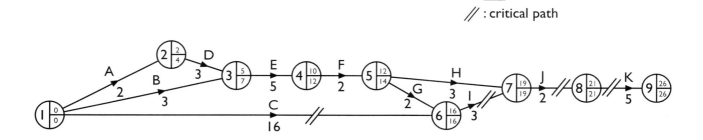

Key
// : critical path

Activity	EST	LFT.	T.F. (LFT – DURATION – EST)
A	0	4	2
B	0	7	4
C	0	16	0
D	2	7	2
E	5	12	2
F	10	14	2
G	12	16	2
H	12	19	4
I	16	19	0
J	19	21	0
K	21	26	0

Figure 9

4 a

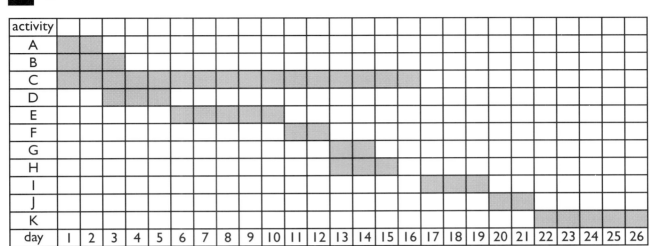

Figure 10 Baden and Clarke's planned production site

b Network analysis and Ghantt charts can improve business decision making in the following ways:

● They are both good planning tools that allow managers to observe a model of how a project will work when it is put into action. The manager can then see how a project will work and what decisions they will need to make in preparation for the project, as well as decisions that will need to be made as the project unfolds. Baden and Clarke will be able to plan at what points they will need to order materials and machinery or organise overtime.

● Network Analysis and Ghantt Charts are useful to managers when they are making decisions as the project unfolds. Managers will know that they have to get certain tasks completed to a certain time, for example those on the critical path. The management at Baden and Clark know that it is vital to make sure that the machinery is installed in three weeks because there is no float on this activity and any delay will prevent the project being completed on time.

● Ghantt Charts and Network Analysis are useful visual tools for managers. By providing a pictorial view of a project they help managers see the whole project and the interrelationships between activities. The managers in Baden and Clarke can clearly see the whole process of building the new production site.

However, it is worth pointing out that all the activities included in the model are set out to last forecasted time periods. In reality these time periods are unlikely to be accurate and this will upset the whole flow of the project. Baden and Clarke may well find that an activity, such as putting on the roof, takes much longer than originally anticipated and this affects the whole running of the project.

Overall, both the Ghantt Chart and Network analysis are useful tools to improve decision making, particularly in the planning stage where their use can considerably improve the efficiency of a project.

UNIT 9 Marketing

QUALITY INNS TEST THE MARKET

Student book pages 229–230

1 A market segment is part of a market made up of consumers with some common characteristic. It could be based on age, sex, socio-economic status, geographical area, etc. Quality Inns target market segment is company executives who are travelling on business. Market segmentation is important because it dictates how each element of the marketing mix will be used by Quality Inns to market their product.
b Mark-up is the addition of profit per unit added to unit cost to give the final selling price for a product. Quality Inns use a mark-up of 200% on variable costs to set a price for its dinner tickets. The mark-up added by a company will vary from industry to industry and depends on how responsive consumers are to price. For example, fashion retailing mark-up tends to be much higher than food retailing because consumers are less responsive to price.
c Variable costs are costs that change with output. As a business produces more, variable costs will increase. Variable costs tend to be direct labour and direct materials where a rise in output means more of these resources needs to be employed. For Quality Inns, food is a variable cost because the more people attend a function the more food Quality Inns will need to purchase.
d A marketing strategy is a plan of how a business will go about successfully marketing its product. Quality Inns will go through the following process to produce a strategy:

- It will conduct an internal and external audit of the present situation affecting Quality Inns.
- It will conduct a SWOT analysis of the situation facing Quality Inns.
- It will make predictive assumptions about how the future might affect the marketing of the product.
- It will set objectives for the marketing of the product by the hotel.
- It will devise strategy of how the marketing mix can be used to market the product successfully.
- After the product has been marketed the results that its achieves will be measured.

2 200% mark-up on variable costs:
£7,50 × 3 = £22.50

b Break-even = fixed cost / selling price − unit variable cost
£1200 / £22.50 − £7.50 = 80 tickets
c

sales	500 @ 22.50	11,250
variable costs	500 @ 7.50	3,750
fixed costs		1,200
total cost		4,950
profit		6,300

Table 31 The maximum Quality Inns hotel profit

3 The marginal cost of the tickets would be £7.50 which covers the cost of each additional ticket sold. This would be the minimum price Quality Inns would set for a discounted ticket. A price that was lower than this would mean a loss would be made on the ticket sold. However, a price of £7.50 would not yield any contribution to fixed costs, so Quality Inns would want to set a price above £7.50 so that the company could make a contribution to fixed costs while retaining a worthwhile discounted price.

b There are a number of other factors that Quality Inns would need to take into account before they set the discounted price:

- If Quality Inns could sell all the tickets for the dinner at the normal price then there would be no point in selling the tickets at the discounted price.
- Quality Inn would need to be aware of views of customers who had paid the full price for the tickets who found out that other customer were paying a discounted price. The customers who paid the full price may not return or would seek a discounted price at a future event.
- Discounting tickets could mean that people come to the dinner who would not have otherwise have come to the hotel. If they like the hotel then they may use it in the future.
- The people who are attracted by the discount may book rooms for the night which means that Quality Inns earn extra revenue from the discount.
- When setting a discounted price the hotel must consider its image; if too much discounting takes place it may adversely affect the image of the Hotel.

Quality Inns needs to make sure that the discounting of tickets is carefully managed to make sure it has a positive not a negative impact on the company's image. In the long term, discounting could damage its reputation and reduce future sales.

4 This is how a market research could be carried out to establish what type of food and drink are wanted at a banquet. It is important to remember that the target market will be people who organise banquets, such as companies and sports clubs, but that the customers will be people who attend the banquet. Thus the research should be targeted at those who attend the banquet because they will be the people who consume the food and drink.

Market research survey on the type of food and drink Quality Inn's customers want at banqueting functions

Objectives

- To produce a survey that allows Quality Inns to analyse their consumers' views on the type of food and drink that they want served at a Quality Inn hotel function.
- To produce an accurate sample of the target market segment.
- To produce a questionnaire that successfully produces information on the views of the target market segment on the food and drink served at a hotel function.

Method of research

Quality Inns should use personal interviews to conduct their research. The company has the resources to conduct this type of research which is time consuming and expensive. However, the personal contact will allow the company to build up a more accurate picture of the consumers' views and it will yield a high response rate. The interviewer will be able to guide the respondent through the questionnaire so that they understand the questions.

Sampling

Quality Inns is a major company that is well resourced and can provide enough finance for the market research project to use random sampling. This will provide a more statistically accurate set of results than the cheaper option of quota sampling. To make sure that the sample produces a statistically meaningful result Quality Inns should sample a large number of customers (several thousand) so that the sample is statistically representative of the target market segment. Respondents would be chosen picking people as they made a reservation. This could be every xth person who made a telephone reservation or came into the hotel to attend a function, eat in the restaurant or take a room. This process would be carried out from a certain number of Quality Inn hotels throughout the country so that the survey is not distorted by a regional bias.

Questionnaire

The aim of the questionnaire is to build up a picture of what consumers who attend a function want in terms of food and drink. Each question must yield information that produces information that will help Quality Inns achieve the objectives set by the survey. The questions must be easy to understand and answer. A mixture of open and closed questions should be used to give both information that is easy to analyse from closed questions, and introduces new ideas from open questions. They should also produce responses that can be analysed to produce the desired information.

Here are some sample questions:

1 When you are eating out formally would you choose a cold starter?

every time ☐ most times ☐ sometimes ☐
rarely ☐ never ☐

This question would be used to see whether customers preferred hot or cold starters. This information would be used to help build up a starter menu that met with consumer tastes. A scaled response is used to make analysis of the questionnaire straightforward.

2 When you are eating out formally what drink do you normally take with your meal?

white wine ☐ red wine ☐
sparkling water ☐ still water ☐ beer ☐
soft drinks ☐ other ☐ (specify)

This question tries to establish the type of drinks that need to be on offer at a banqueting event.

3 When you eat out formally how much would you normally expect to pay for a bottle of wine?

£7–£9 ☐ £9–£12 ☐ £12–£15 ☐
£15–£18 ☐ £18+ ☐

This question seeks to establish how much consumers will pay for a bottle of wine. This will provide some data on the quality of wine that consumers would expect at a Banquet.

Conclusion

The research on the food and drink that the consumers want would need to be part of a complete piece of research on banqueting. The research should use:

- personal interviews
- random sampling of the target market
- structured questionnaire with a mixture of open and closed questions.

---

5 **a** A promotional mix is the types of promotional techniques that Quality Inns could use to promote its product. It would be the mix of above the line promotion, such as advertising in newspapers and magazines, and below the line methods, such as point of sale material, mailshots and consumer incentives.

b In deciding on a promotional mix it is important first to consider who the target market segment is and then choose a mix of techniques that would give exposure to this segment. In this case the target segment would be companies, sports clubs, charities or any organisation that is interested in holding a function. The target market would be people who organise dinners. The promotion could take two basic forms. Firstly, it needs to be in a place to inform people who are specifically looking to organise a function that Quality Inns offers such a facility. Secondly it needs to attract people who may not be organising at the time but may do so in the future:

- Using trade magazines would be a type of advertising that would come to the attention of people within companies who organise dinners.
- Using sports magazines, such as *Golf Monthly*, to advertise would reach people at sports clubs.
- Local newspapers could make the banqueting facilities available those in the local community who would want banqueting facilities.
- Mailshots to sports clubs and social clubs within companies would reach the target segment.
- Point of sale advertising, where there are brochures and leaflets advertising functions in the hotel rooms and reception would come to the attention of people staying in the hotels.
- *Yellow Pages*, *Thompson Directory*, and *Talking Pages* would be above the line advertising that would come to the attention of people looking for hotels that organise functions.
- An Internet website is a growing form of above the line promotion that could be used to target those who are looking to organise a function.

YOUTH APPEAL - MOTORING : WHY ROVER TRANSFORMED THE METRO

Student book pages 230–231

1   **a** Open or unstructured questions allow the respondent to express themselves as fully as they wish in whatever way they think is suitable. In Rover's case, it would be a question that asked the respondent what attracted them to Rover cars. The respondent would be free to express their reply in their own way. A closed or structured question only allows the respondent to give a set answer. For example, Rover might ask a respondent whether they thought Rover cars were reliable, offering a fixed response of yes or no.
b A questionnaire that is made up of closed questions would have the advantage being easy to analyse. Each question would have a set limit of responses which could be fed into a computer to give precise statistics to summarise the findings of the questionnaire. It would give figures on the colours that people prefer, what size engines they buy, where they purchase their cars, whether they buy news cars or not and how often they change their car. This means that a statistical profile can be drawn up for each customer which can then be used in the next stage of the marketing process.
c The problem with closed questionnaires is that they will only throw up ideas that have been considered by the company. To introduce new ideas, and truly look at things from the perspective of the respondent, Rover would need to use open questions. For example, a closed question might not bring up an idea like the fact that young people see the

Metro's image as rather old fashioned and lacking a 'cool' image. This type of information would be vital to any marketing plan that involved trying to introduce younger age groups to Rover cars. Attitudes and feelings are far better expressed through the consumers' own words than in set responses.

2 **a** Socio-economic grouping involves separating people according to characteristics such as income, wealth, career/job and education. Separating people into socio-economic groups is one method by which businesses can segment their markets. In the market research carried out by Rover the socio-economic grouping of people who were surveyed was recorded.

b Rover would find it useful to divide their market up into socio economic groups for the following reasons;

● Grouping consumers according to their socio-economic status is one way in which Rover can successfully segment their market. Knowledge of the income, education and work of their target market segment will tell Rover about what their consumers might want from a car. Cars are a status symbol and people want the type of car they drive to reflect their status within their socio-economic group. For example, the Rover car targeted at the AB socio-economic group, needs to have the quality and image that reflects the aspirations of people in this group. Rover then needs to adjust each element of the marketing mix to persuade this group of consumers to buy their cars. This means that the design of the product, its advertising, price and distribution all need to meet with the desires of consumers in the socio-economic group AB.

● Grouping on the basis of socio-economic status will help Rover in its market research. If most consumers fall into the ABC1 category then these are the people who need to be sampled in any market research, because these are the people who are most likely to buy Rover cars.

Rover does have to be careful when segmenting people according to socio-economic grouping because people do not necessarily fit neatly into the various groups. The characteristics of each group can be misleading. For example, people with relatively little formal education earn very high salaries. In any marketing plan Rover should be careful to allow for this.

3 The most frequently occurring salary is the range £25,001–£30,000.

b The salary or incomes of Rover's consumers is very important in the marketing of Rover cars because it has a major impact on the amount of money consumers have to buy Rover cars. This in turn is an influence on the prices that Rover can charge for their car. Rover will organise finance arrangements for people to buy their cars which will be affected by the consumers income. Average salary is another factor that can be used by Rover when they are segmenting their market.

4 Products should be designed with the following factors in mind; function, economic viability and aesthetics.

Function is important in the design of a Rover car in the following ways:

● **Performance:** Rover cars should achieve a certain quality in terms of speed, acceleration, cornering.
● **Comfort:** the quality of the upholstery, seats, the amount of leg room and smoothness of ride should all achieve a certain level in a Rover car.
● **Safety:** seat belts and impact bars would be part of the design of the car to ensure its safety.
● **Reliability:** this is a major thing that car buyers want from their cars.

Economic viability is important because:

● If the Rover does not perform its function effectively then people will not buy the car. Thus it is a vital part of product design. However, its effectiveness must be achieved at a price the consumer can afford. If the final price of the car means that consumers cannot afford it then its design is not effective. A price of £6,495 is at a level that will attract the target market.

Aesthetics is important because:

- Aesthetics is very important in car design. The look of the Rover is a vital part of its design.

- For example, the need to have a sleek demand to attract the target consumer.

It is the balance of these three elements that needs to be achieved for the Rover 100 to be a successful product. If the price is low, but the car does not meet certain standards in terms of function then the product will not be successful.

NIKE OUTSPRINTS ITS RIVALS

Student book pages 232–233

1   **a**   Market share is the proportion of total market sales accounted for by one company's product or products. For example, if Nike training shoes sales in the UK were £500m and total market sales were £1,000m then Nike would have a 50% market share of the UK training shoe market.

Market growth is the increase in total sales of the entire market over time. For example, if the global sports shoe market increased from £10.7 billion to £12 billion then this would be market growth.

     b   As Nike's sports shoe sales have increased worldwide over the last few years its share of the world sports shoe market has increased.

     c   Nike's world market share of the sports shoe market:

$$£3.2B / £10.7B \times 100 = 29.9\%$$

     d   Most of the growth in the training shoe market has come from emerging markets in Asia and South America.

     e   There will be a number of difficulties for Nike as it tries to expand into developing countries:

- There are cultural and language difficulties that have to be overcome. Markets in developing countries may not accept the marketing techniques used by Nike as it tries to expand. The names of products might have to be changed and style of the shoes altered to meet differences in local tastes. However, the image of Nike is a global one and many people in developing markets aspire to own western products because their image represents economic progress and wealth.
- Distribution in developing countries can be a problem because of poorly developed infrastructure which increases distribution costs. The chain of distribution from the manufacture to the retailer may not be particularly well developed. However, Nike could be able to overcome this by setting up its own lines of distribution using cheap, skilled labour.
- The economies of developing countries tend to be subject to instability. High inflation and a volatile currency can make the trading environment uncertain and expensive to market in. However, this instability can bring about huge upswings in demand which can make the markets extremely lucrative.
- Many developing countries suffer from poor liquidity because of a

shortage of currency (particularly foreign currency) which makes it more difficult for Nike to get paid.

There are significant short term costs in terms of marketing and distribution that Nike will encounter as it tries to increase sales in developing countries. It will also have the constant threat posed by economic instability in the longer term. However, Nike does have the reputation and scale of operation to cope with these problems.

2 a The Boston Matrix is a model that can be used to analyse Nike's product mix using market share and market growth. Each product can be put into a different section of the matrix depending on its market share and market growth rate. A product like Nike Air Michael Jordan basketball shoes would be a cash cow product because of its low market growth buts it high market share.

	high market share	low market share
high market growth	star	problem child
low market growth	cash cow	dog

The product life cycle graphs the profit made by a product during its life. The diagram shows how a Nike brand, such as its running shoes moves through development, introduction, growth, maturity and decline phases of the life cycle. This model again allows Nike to analyse its product mix through the different stages in the life cycle each product has achieved.

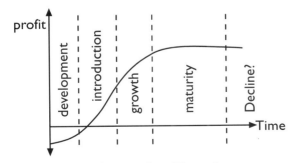

Figure 11 Nike: product life cycle

b To manage its product mix or portfolio most effectively Nike would need to achieve a balance between yielding as much profit as possible from the portfolio against the need to have new products in a position to replace older products when they decline. The Product Life Cycle and Boston Matrix are useful because:

● They allow managers to see where products are in terms of generating profit and cashflow for the business, as well as cashflow to develop other products in the portfolio which may be in the early stages in the life cycle. A cash cow such as Nike Air Jordans could be used to support the development of Nike golf shoes.

● It is vital that Nike has products spread throughout the Product Life Cycle and Boston Matrix so that new products are in position to become the stars and cash cows of the present. If Nike has two many products in the mature phase of the life cycle or as cash cows then once these products decline there is nothing to replace them.

● The Models can be used as an aid to marketing planning. Nike will need to know when it needs to increase expenditure on advertising and promotion, or when to redesign the product, or even to increase price to yield greater profit from a product. For example, Nike Air Jordans may need to be redesigned to extend their maturity and their position as a cash cow.

The most important use of the Product Life Cycle and the Boston Matrix is as a way of managing their portfolio to reduce risk, which is important in ensuring the long term success of the business.

c To extend the life cycle of a product Nike will have to change different aspects of the products marketing mix to try and increase sales and profits. This is an example of how Nike might has extended the life its brand of soccer boots that have started to decline:

- Nike should conduct a marketing audit to see what internal and external factors are affecting the profits of the product and causing it to decline. The decline could be caused by increased competition or a change in taste.
- A SWOT analysis should then be used to examine the internal strengths and weaknesses of the product and the external opportunities and threats faced by the product. For example, the outdated design of Nike's soccer boots could be causing a decline in sales. The opportunity could be to bring out a changed design that would keep the boot up with current tastes.
- Predictive assumptions are made about the future environment and how this might effect the redesigned boot. An assumption may be that a new design will match the tastes and preferences of consumers over next year.
- Objectives should be set for the extension of the product. This could be to increase sales by 10% on the current year.
- The strategy that is going to be used will be based around each element of the marketing mix. The redesigned boot will achieve a certain product quality, it will be given a new image through advertising and promotion, its price will be changed to reflect the new image and the way it is distributed could be altered.
- Finally a process of review should be set up to evaluate the extension strategy that has been implemented. This would take place at a set time after the redesigned boot has been launched.

3 **a** SWOT analysis is a way of analysing the internal and external position of a business, product or division. The strengths and weaknesses of a business are the internal influences that affect the business in the present and the opportunities and threat are the external factors that will affect the business in the present and the future. A company like Nike would use a SWOT analysis as part of its marketing planning process. The model is a useful presentation tool at a management meeting.

b

A SWOT ANALYSIS FOR NIKE AS IT TRIES TO INCREASE SALES IN DEVELOPING COUNTRIES

Strengths:

- The business has an incredibly powerful brand name and image that will attract sales throughout the world.
- Nike has the experience and resources to extend their brands into new markets.
- The company has a dynamic management team that has the ability to make the most of a new market.

Weaknesses

- Nike does not have experience of certain newly emerging markets.
- There is the danger of complacency amongst management. Success in one market does not necessarily guarantee success in another very different market.

MARKETING

Opportunities

- The sales and profits potential of a newly emerging market is huge.
- There will the the opportunity to spread risks across more markets.

Threats

- The marketing environment is different. Decisions that have worked before may not work with a different culture and language.
- Companies like Adidas and Reebok will also be trying to force their way into these new markets.

c

A MARKETING STRATEGY FOR NIKE INTRODUCING A NEW BRAND OF TRAINING SHOE INTO THE CHINESE MARKET

- A marketing audit should be conducted of Nike in respect of the Chinese market. This should summarise where the business is at the present. As a major company marketing training shoes through out the world it is in a strong position to move into the Chinese market.
- A SWOT analysis should be used which will show how much potential there is in the Chinese market, as the country with the highest population that has yet to be exploited by western companies. However, Nike's inexperience in China and the sheer size of the market could be a considerable threat. Indeed the size of the market means that Nike should only try to market their shoes in one region first.
- Predictive assumptions should be made about the state of the market when the training shoes will be sold; essentially, that this market will experience considerable growth over the next few years.
- The marketing mix should be targeted at the Chinese market in the following way. The shoe should be a carefully researched and tested design that will be attractive to Chinese consumers. The product should be promoted through selected promotion channels that will achieve wide coverage in a specific region of the country. The price of the shoes should reflect local incomes and spending patterns. The product should be distributed through Chinese wholesalers who know and understand the market.
- A review process should be set up to evaluate the lessons learned from marketing the product in a particular region of China to see what improvement could be made when the shoe is marketed in other areas.

SPONSORSHIP BY COCA COLA

Student book pages 233–234

1 a Above the line promotion means using an outside medium, where the business does not have direct control, to carry out the business's promotion. This would be the use of a newspaper, television channel, radio station or bill board to carry the promotion. Above the line promotion would be TV advertising by Coca Cola.

Below the line promotion is where the firm has more direct control over the promotion that takes place. This would be a mailshot by a business, or the use of point of sale materials. The Coca Cola signs that appear in shops, bars and restaurants that serve Coca Cola are below the line promotion.

   b Sponsorship such as Coca Cola's endorsement of soccer and the Olympics is a form of below the line promotion because the company has direct control over the promotion that takes place. It decides what events to sponsor, and the way the event is sponsored. However, to an extent the impact of this type of promotion occurs through television which has the characteristics of above the line promotion.
   c Two other methods of below the line promotion that Coca Cola would use would be:

   ● Immediate consumer incentives, where the product is sold with a percentage of extra Coca Cola in the can or bottle. For example, a oversized can would carry the slogan 20% extra free. In this case the consumer receives the benefits of the promotion as they buy the product.
   ● Delayed consumer incentives, where a competition is printed on the back of a Coca Cola can. In this case, the benefits of the promotion are saved until some point in the future. This type of promotion is often used to gain repeat purchases.

2 Coca Cola's association with sport would have enhanced its image because many of the positive images that are displayed in sport are those that Coca Cola would want to be associated with. These include:

   ● youth
   ● achievement
   ● health
   ● vitality
   ● clean living
   ● success.

The sports that Coca Cola has chosen also attract a huge amount of interest and are covered extensively by television and newspapers. Many of the people who take part in sport are role models that people look up to and follow. It is very attractive to have Coca Cola associated with these types of people.

   b As a method of promotion, sponsorship will enhance the image of the Coca Cola in the long term. There is no specific attempt to sell the product immediately, as might be the case with some form of special offer or a concentrated TV advertising campaign. As Coca Cola's image is enhanced in the eyes of the consumer more people will consume the product. As the sales of the product rise, revenue and profits will increase. Because sponsorship enhances the image of the product in the long term, sales will probably not fall back after a period of time as they might do with a short term promotional campaign.
   c The sports that Coca Cola has chosen could have be selected for the following reasons:

   ● The Olympics is arguably the biggest single global sports event that takes place. The coverage that Coca Cola receives from its sponsorship of the event is huge in terms of exposure to consumers world wide. The Olympics has an international image that breaks down national boundaries, an image that Coca Cola wants for its product.
   ● Football, as a world game, also gives Coca Cola a global image and provides massive exposure worldwide. Unlike the Olympics, soccer is played every year and throughout the year, so it provides ever-present exposure for Coca Cola. Football introduces the idea of support and loyalty to a team; Coca Cola wants to attract this type of loyalty to its brand.
   ● Coca Cola used the sponsorship of tennis to promote Diet Coca Cola with the intention of targeting young

women. Tennis is a very popular sport amongst women and Wimbledon is also probably one of the biggest women's sporting events that attracts world media attention.

- The Special Olympics possibly would have been an ethical decision for Coca Cola. It would certainly have given the company a caring public image. The decision to sponsor the event possibly would not have been done on commercial grounds, but rather on ethical grounds.

The key theme behind all Coca Cola's sponsorship is the desire to achieve global coverage using events that have a wide mix of nationalities. This portrays an image that is behind the whole philosophy of the brand name Coca Cola.

UNIT 10

The business environment – Section A: The market

THE CLASSICAL MUSIC BUSINESS

Student book pages 249–251

1 a The following factors will influence the demand for a product:

- **The price of the product:** if prices fall demand tends to increase.
- **The price of related products:** if complements fall in price, or substitutes rise in price then the demand for a product will increase.
- **Income of consumers:** for normal goods, there is a positive relationship between demand and consumer income.
- **Consumer taste:** if taste and fashion changes in favour of a product then the demand for it will tend to increase.
- **Future price expectations:** this tends only to apply to assets, such as houses, where if the price of the product is expected to rise in the future demand for the product will increase in the present.
- **Consumer confidence:** if consumers feel confident about the security of their future financial position they will increase the demand for products in the present.
- **Interest rates:** if interest rates fall the demand for products that are typically bought on credit tend to rise.
- **Wealth:** if people's wealth increases when asset prices rise, like a rise in house prices, then they will increase their demand for products.

b

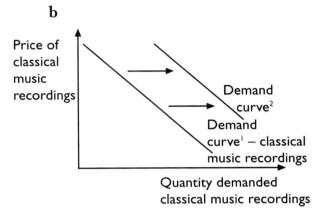

Figure 12 An increase in demand for classical music recordings

c According to the case study, sales of classical music has increased from $9B to $20B from 1980 to 1992. Thus the demand for classical music CDs has increased. The factors that have led to this increase are:

- **Consumer taste:** the following factors have caused the demand for consumer taste to change in favour of classical music; musicians such as Nigel Kennedy and Pavarotti have become increasingly popular, the quality of CDs is better than the quality of vinyl and is better suited to classical music and people have rebuilt their classical music collections in CD format.
- **Population:** the ageing population has led to an increase in the demand for classical music.
- **The price of the product:** as the price of classical CDs has fallen the demand for them has increased.
- **Consumer income:** as consumer incomes rise the demand for classical CDS increase because it is a normal good where demand is positively related to income.

- **Related goods:** as the price of CD players falls there is an increase in the demand for CDs; a complementary relationship.

2 a The supply curve graphs the relationship between the quantity supplied of a product and its price. The diagram below illustrates the supply schedule for classical music CDs.

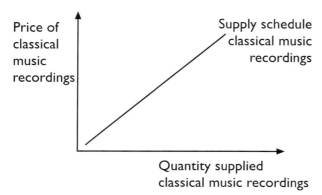

Figure 13 The supply schedule for classical music recordings

b The supply schedule is upward sloping with a positive relationship between the price of classical music CDs and their price. It is a positive relationship because as prices increase, the profit that the producers can make from producing CDs also increases so the firms produce more.

c As the demand for classical music recordings has increased producers in the industry will have produced more and increased the amount they supply. This will not cause a shift in the supply curve but a movement along the supply curve takes place. As new firms have entered the market the supply curve would have shifted to the right. The development of new technology in the industry will have allowed producers to produce more at each given price, again causing the supply curve to shift to the right. The use of low cost labour by companies like Naxos would also have caused the supply curve to shift to the right.

3 A manager of a small chain of record shops should stock the following types of classical music:

- The work of popular classical musicians, such as Nigel Kennedy and the Three Tenors, would attract much of the new demand for popular classical music that has come from new, younger buyers.
- To attract the passionate enthusiasts the record shop should stock a wide selection of recordings from lesser known composers.
- Occasional customers would be attracted by a selection of well known material from music and television.
- Traditional buyers need to be attracted by a wide range of traditional classical music who will want to replace their outdated vinyl collections.
- New buyers could also be attracted by carrying the budget recording produced by the Naxos label.

4 The advantages for a record company that specialises in popular music moving into the production of classical recordings:

- The market for classical music is growing which means that the potential sales and profits that can be generated from the market will be good.
- There is potential to move into the market at a low cost by following the example of Naxos, who have illustrated how classical music can gain a high market share producing budget CDs.
- By diversifying into classical music the record company will be spreading its risks. If the demand for the popular music they produce falls then it can be made up for through the sales of classical music.
- Expanding into classical music will allow the record company to increase the scale of its production which will give it greater economies of scale. For example, it will be able to buy capital and materials in bulk which will give them lower unit costs.

However, there are disadvantages associated with the diversification into this new market:

- The record company does not have experience in classical recording. This lack of experience may adversely affect the quality of the product they produce and their costs of production.
- Expansion can lead to diseconomies of scale which arise from the expansion of the company. A new classical music division might make the whole process of managing the organisation more difficult.
- The record company will be competing with experienced producers of classical music who may have the knowledge to out-compete the company.
- When markets grow very quickly, it is possible that at some point the market might experience some contraction. If the company has to invest a large sum of funds in the classical music market and there was a decline, then there could be a risk of losing the funds.

In the short term, there will be quite substantial set up costs associated with moving into the classical music market. The company may also find it initially difficult to establish itself in the market because of a lack of experience. However, in the long term, there is the potential to spread risks and increase sales.

COFFEE FROST DAMAGE PUT AT 40%

Student book page 252

1 The diagram shows how the coffee frost damage has caused the supply curve for coffee on the London Commodity Exchange to shift to the left. This causes the price of coffee to rise on the Exchange.

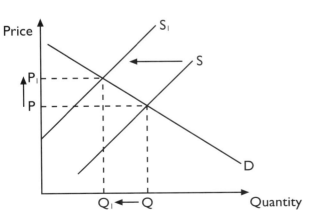

Figure 14 A fall in coffee supply as a result of frost damage

2 a As the price of coffee increases, the cost of buying coffee from the Exchange by the instant coffee producer will rise, which leads to a rise in direct costs for the producer. The coffee producer then has the decision of whether to pass on the increase in costs in the form of higher prices or accept a reduction in its profit margins. The decision as to whether to pass on the price increase to the final consumer will depend on the price elasticity of demand for coffee amongst final consumers. If the demand for coffee is price inelastic then the rise in price will mean that the company will be able to maintain its revenue levels after the price increase. However, if the demand of its consumers is price elastic then the rise in price will cause a large fall in demand and a substantial drop in revenue. If the rise in coffee price means that prices have to be increased and demand for the company's instant coffee falls then the company may have to reduce the numbers of people they employ.

b This is a strategy that a coffee producer could use to deal with the problem caused by the rise in coffee prices.

- To start with the company could look for alternative sources of coffee supply. This would mean buying coffee from a country other than Brazil and by-passing the London Coffee Exchange. However, because the fall in Brazilian supply will cause the world supply to fall, general coffee prices worldwide might have increased which would mean that the option of obtaining coffee at a lower price would be restricted.
- The next thing the company could do would be to try and hold other costs down. This could mean trying to reduce labour costs and other material costs. The company could also aim to increase productivity to keep unit costs down. This would mean the company may not have to pass on the whole price increase.
- In the pricing decision, the company needs to decide how much of the increase in the cost of the coffee to pass on in the form of higher prices. In making the pricing decision, the company should make an assessment of its coffee's price elasticity of demand. If the company wants to maintain its sales volume it will need accept a lower profit margin from its coffee sales.
- Finally, to support the sales of its coffee the company could use extensive sales promotion. This could mean using an advertising campaign that emphasises the quality of the coffee they produce and takes the consumer's mind away from the higher price.

UNIT 10

The business environment – Section B: The macroeconomy

THE CHINA COMPANY LTD ATTEMPT TO MAINTAIN MARGINS

Student book page 263

1 a Economic growth is the rise in an economy's real national income over time. The national income is measured by the economy's Gross Domestic Product (GDP) which is the money value of goods and services produced by the economy. Economic growth is measured by the percentage annual change in the economy's GDP. The China Company operates in an economy where GDP will be growing at an annual rate of 3%.

b As the economy grows, people will receive higher incomes and have more money to spend on goods and services. This may well mean an increase in the demand for the goods and services produced by The China Company. The increase in demand will depend on the income elasticity of demand for the products that The China Company produces. If the income elasticity of demand for The China Company's products is positive then demand for their products will rise.

c The finance director of The China Company believes that the rise in demand for its product brought about by economic growth of 3% will be 8%. This is an income elasticity of demand of:

$$8/3 = 2.67$$

This means that the goods produced by The China Company are luxury products because a rise in consumer income brings about a larger percentage rise in demand for the product.

2 The China Company's projected profit and loss account for the year ending 31 December 1998.

	£'000' 1997	£'000' 1998
sales	1,800 × 1.08	1,944
direct costs	700 × 1.15	805
gross profit	1,100	1,139
overheads	400 × 0.98	392
net profit	700	747

Table 32 Budgeted profit and loss account for The China Company

3 a There are two reasons why direct costs might be projected to increase in the forecasted profit and loss account:

● As output increases to meet the rise in demand The China Company would need to buy in more raw materials and more labour which would cause the direct costs to rise.

● The price for each unit of direct costs could increase as the economy expands. This is because all the firms in the China manufacturing market will be looking to buy more raw materials and hire more labour. As the demand for both raw materials and labour increases its price may well rise, increasing The China Company's direct costs.

b The Company could try to hold down the rise in direct labour costs in the following ways:

● The existing labour force could be asked to increase its productivity to meet the increase in demand. Increasing productivity means raising the level of output per unit of labour input. This could mean employing new production methods and using more up to date technology. If the productivity of the workers increases then the unit costs of each additional output may fall. However, to do this The China Company will need to have the co-operation of the labour force, who must be motivated to increase their productivity. This could be done using bonuses (Mcgregor's Theory X) of by reorganising workers into teams and giving them a greater say in production decision making (Mcgregor's Theory Y)

- Direct labour costs could be held down by replacing the labour with capital. Machinery could be used to make their china products. However, this would mean making workers redundant which could lead to a drop in morale in the company and lead to industrial conflict. There would also be the high initial costs of employing new machinery. It may also not be all that easy to replace workers with capital.

In the short term, employing new methods in production to raise productivity and or employing capital in place of labour may actually lead to a rise in costs. The benefits in terms of lower unit costs are more likely to be felt in the long term.

4 The finance director is concerned that rise in output by The China Company will lead to a fall in profit margins. To try and maintain margins by increasing price the company will have the following problems:

- There could be a great deal of competition facing The China Company in the market for its products. This would mean that the price elasticity of demand for the company's products would be price elastic. If the company tried to increase its price to increase profit margins then its revenue would fall which would lead to a lower reported net and gross profit.
- Increasing prices may upset some of The China Company's long term customers who might take their business somewhere else in response to the rise in price. This would adversely affect the long term profitability of the company.

Reducing costs can be done by increasing productivity which means increasing output per unit of input and reducing unit costs. This could be done by developing new production systems and creating incentives for the workforce to raise productivity. It could also be done by replacing labour with capital. However, there are problems with this approach which may lead to redundancies which in turn could lead to a fall in morale amongst the labour force at The China Company and even industrial conflict.

The China Company could try and reduce costs by looking for new raw material suppliers that can supply at a lower cost. However, if the economy is expanding and there is a high demand for raw materials the company might find it difficult to find cheaper alternatives.

CONSTRUCTION INDUSTRY STEEPED IN GLOOM

Student book pages 264–265

1 a The main characteristics of an economic recession are:

- Slow or negative economic growth which means that peoples incomes only grow very slowly.

- Falling profits and business failure because falling incomes means that the demand for goods and services falls.
- Rising unemployment as businesses fail and other business reduce output as demand in the economy falls.

- Low inflation as firms hold prices constant or even reduce prices as demand falls.

These are the characteristics of the construction industry as it experienced recession in the early 1990s. For example, the there was an 8.5 % reduction in construction industry output during the recession that occurred in the UK in 1991.

b The construction industry is affected by recession more than other industries such as food and energy for the following reasons:

- Buildings are a major item of expenditure for businesses that are buying new premises and people buying houses. When there is a recession businesses and individuals will put off such major items of expenditure which means there is a major fall in the demand for the products produced by construction firms.
- Businesses and people often need to borrow a large amount of money to finance the acquisition of a building. They do not like to commit themselves to borrowing when the economy is in recession.
- Generally speaking, it is not a necessity for businesses to move into new premises and people into new houses. These are transactions that people can put off when the economic environment is depressed. By putting off these transactions there will be a fall in the demand for the products produced by construction companies.

Food and energy expenditure that are necessities that cannot be put off until some point in the future and does not represent the huge initial expenditure that is needed when a building is purchased. Thus the demand for food and energy is not as responsive to changes in economic growth as construction is.

2 The case study says that profit margins in the brick industry have been squeezed by a price war in the brick market. This would mean that the price of bricks has fallen as firms in the industry have increased supply. In the recession the fall in demand for construction products would mean there would be a subsequent fall in the demand for bricks. The diagram shows how an increase in supply and a fall in demand will cause a fall in the price of bricks.

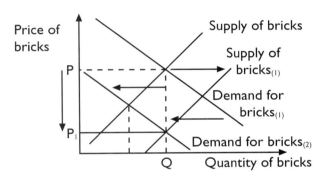

Figure 15 A supply and demand analysis of the price of bricks

3 **a** The economic recession of the early 1990s will have the following effects on Aspect Carpets:

- Because fewer people and businesses are moving house there will be a fall in demand for carpets. Demand will also fall because people and businesses will have less money to spend on furnishings. The fall in demand means that Aspect Carpets will experience a fall in sales and a fall in profits.
- When demand falls in a recession businesses tend to take longer to pay their debts as their finances are put under greater pressure. If one firm takes longer to pay then this tends to set off a chain reaction because the supplier they delay payment to will then delay payment to their supplier and so on. In addition, as businesses go bankrupt in a recession there is a rise of bad debt. The rise in bad debts and late

payment means that Aspect Carpets is likely to suffer a fall in liquidity.
- As the market for carpets becomes more depressed in a recession, Aspect Carpets will need to reduce prices and offer discounts to maintain sales. As the company reduces prices, their profit margins will fall.
- As unemployment rises, Aspect Carpets will find it easier to recruit the staff they need. The company will find that its staff become more concerned with keeping their jobs and become easier to manage. The turnover of staff at Aspect Carpets is likely to fall as the workforce find it more difficult to find new jobs outside the company.

The most dangerous problem that Aspect Carpets is likely to face in a recession is the pressure that will be put on its cashflow. Small and medium sized companies often fail in a recession when they run out of cash.

A strategy that Aspect Carpets could use to try and deal with the threats posed by an economic recession

- It is important that Aspect Carpets sets itself clear objective about how it is going to deal with the recession and what are the most important parts of its business it should concentrate on.
- As the demand for its carpets falls, the company should try to maintain its own sales by discounting and by improving the quality of its service.
- In a recession, the demand for cheaper carpets with a low income elasticity of demand will possibly hold up better than more expensive carpets with a high income elasticity of demand. Aspect Carpets should increase its stocks of this type of carpet during a recession.
- To maintain its profit margins it is important that Aspect Carpets controls its costs carefully. This can be done by negotiating low cost deals with its suppliers of raw materials and by not paying high wage increases.
- To protect its cashflow position the company should produce careful cashflow projections, so that they know when the company will come under cashflow pressure. They can use the cash budget to plan for the organisation of funds needed to cover any shortfall in cash.
- Aspect Carpets must develop a clear policy to deal with late payment and the threat of bad debt. The company must make sure that it chases up individuals and companies that do not pay on time. It may also need to make arrangement to factor certain debts.
- Aspect Carpets must carefully communicate with the workforce the strategy that is going to be implemented so that the whole organisation works in the same direction to deal with the threat of recession. For example, workers must be told why their wages may well be held down.

It is very important for the long term survival of Aspect Carpets that the company has a strategy with clear objectives, that deals with each threat that a recession poses to it, and that it is communicated with the whole organisation.

UNIT 10
The business environment – Section C: International business

CASPER AND SONS IN EUROPE?

Student book pages 272–273

A report on the advantages and disadvantages of marketing their toys in Europe

To: The directors of Casper and Sons

These are the advantages of Casper and Sons marketing their toys in Europe:

- Europe is a huge market with a large number of potential consumers that Casper and Sons could sell their toys to. The sales that the European market could generate for the company could greatly increase the company's turnover and profits.
- If the sales increase then Casper will be able to produce more toys. As the company produces more toys, it will increase the scale of its production which will lead to economies of scale and reduce its unit costs. For example, the company will be able to increase the scale of the machinery it uses which will give the company technical economies.
- By concentrating on the domestic market, Casper and Sons will put itself in a vulnerable situation if there was a fall in demand in the domestic market. Marketing in Europe means that the company will be spreading its risks across different markets which would make up for a fall in demand in the home market.
- Entering the European market will mean that the company will pick up new ideas from European toy firms on product design, marketing and production. This will help Casper and Sons improve their long term performance.

However there are a number of disadvantages associated with marketing their products in Europe:

- The company will be entering a market that is new to Casper and Sons and one the company has little experience of. The tastes of consumers in the European toy market will be different from the UK, and this means that many of their products would need to be changed or redesigned.
- Marketing in Europe means that Casper and Sons will have to deal with the problem of the exchange rate. To start with there is the conversion cost of changing currencies and then the prices set will be affected by changes in the exchange rate.
- Marketing products when there are language and cultural barriers to overcome is difficult. Brand names, promotional campaigns all need to be changed to allow for these differences.
- By entering Europe, Casper and Sons will be extending its organisation which could lead to diseconomies of scale. Managing an organisation which sells in international markets can be more difficult in terms of communication.
- Entering Europe will increase the business's distribution costs. If it produces the products in the UK and exports them to Europe it will have to pay to get the products to the market. The company could use a European agent to sell their products, although it will lose some control over the marketing of the product if it does this.
- Casper will come up against local manufactures within Europe who will be resistant to their entry. Certain European retailers may be reluctant to sell Casper's products for fear of upsetting local producers.

Conclusion

Casper and Sons entry into Europe carries significant problems in the short term. It may take time for the company to penetrate the market and set up effective lines of distribution. However, in the long term the scale of the market in terms of potential sales gives the business significant opportunities for growth.

2

A marketing strategy for Casper and Sons as they prepare to sell their product in Europe

- The company needs to conduct an internal and external audit of their current situation to see the company's position in relation to exporting into Europe. The internal audit considers the company's qualities as a firm in terms of their ability to export into Europe. The external audit would consider the market conditions within Europe and how this might affect Casper and Sons as they market their product in Europe.
- The marketing audit can be built on by using a SWOT analysis. This involves taking the information that has been produced by the marketing audit and summarising it in terms of the strengths and weaknesses the company has and the opportunities and threats that are present in the market. The strength of Casper and Sons is their experience in producing a high quality product. Its weakness is its lack of experience in marketing its product in overseas markets. The opportunities offered by the European market are the huge number of consumers the market will offer the company. The markets threat is the fact that the company has to overcome the problem of the exchange rate.
- Predictive assumptions about what may happen in the future that will affect Casper and Sons when it markets its product in Europe will have to be made. The company would need to assume that monetary union will take place and consider how this will affect the marketing of the toys in Europe.
- Casper and Sons will need to set objectives that it wants to achieve from the marketing of the toys in Europe. This would involve setting targets for where the company wants to go. This could be supported by the use of the Ansoff's matrix which summarises the risks associated with the different directions the company could go in. They would also need set objectives for the sales, market share, cashflow, and profits that Casper and Son's want to achieve.
- Once the objectives are in place the company needs to devise the strategy. This involves setting each element of the marketing mix to achieve the objectives set successfully. The product that Caspers produces will need to be of a quality and design to attract European consumers. A price needs to be set that covers the cost of producing the product, and attracts European consumers. The type of promotion chosen must be one that is suitable for the European market, using local advertising mediums to gain access to European consumers. The choice of distribution channel to market the toys needs to be made. This would could involve using a local agent within the local European market to distribute to retailers in the market.
- Finally Casper and Sons will need to set up a procedure for reviewing the results of marketing the product in Europe. This procedure should be based on the objectives set in the marketing strategy.

THE BUSINESS ENVIRONMENT – SECTION C: INTERNATIONAL BUSINESS

CLOCKWISE LTD DEAL WITH EXCHANGE RATES

Student book pages 273–274

1 a Clockwise would have chosen to move its production to China because of the cost advantages the company could gain from producing in China. This is because the cost of labour is much lower in China than in the UK. The company will also not have the costs running and maintaining a production plant.

b There are a number of problems that Clockwise will encounter when it out-sources production to China:

- The company will have pay for the product in Chinese Yen. Thus it will encounter the commission expense of exchanging currencies. Clockwise will also have to deal with the problem of changes in the exchange rate. If the Pound falls against the Chinese Yen then the cost of units bought in will increase.
- There are certain risks associated with the quality of the product bought in from China. The quality of the out-sourced unit my not be as high as the product that Clockwise produced itself.
- Because the unit is being produced on the other side of the world there is a problem with communication. The language and culture are different in China which means that it may be difficult for Clockwise to deal with its Chinese supplier.
- Clockwise will have to pay, directly or indirectly, the transport cost of moving the input from China to the UK.
- The Chinese supplier will work towards its own objectives which may not be the same as Clockwise. The loyalty that exists between the production site owned by the company will be higher than that of the Chinese supplier.

2 a 14 Yen to £1: £2.00 × 14 = 28 Yen
b Chinese Yen rise from 14 : £1 to 15 : £1

The price of the unit is assumed to remain at 28Y

therefore 28Y/15 = £1.87

selling price − unit direct cost = contribution
£14.99 − £1.87 = £13.12

3 a Calculating revenue = price × quantity sold

revenue in £s:
£14.99 × 500,000 = £7,495,000

revenue (9FF:£1) in FF:
£7,495,000 × 9FF = 67,455,000FF

b Revenue in £s:
£14.99 × 450,000 = £6,745,500

revenue (10FF:£1) in FF
£6,745,500 × 10FF = 67,455,000FF

4

A report on a strategy for dealing with a rise in the value of Sterling

To: the directors of Clockwise Ltd

Impact of a rise in Sterling

As the value of the Pound rises against the value of other foreign currencies the price of Clockwise products will become more expensive on foreign markets. This is because foreign buyers have to buy Sterling, which has become more expensive to them, in order to buy Clockwise's products. In the example of Sterling rising from 9FF:£1 to 10FF:£1, the price of a watch has increased from 134.91FF (9FF × £14.99) to 149.90FF (10FF × £14.99), which leads to a fall in the demand for the watches in France. In this case revenue has not fallen, but if the fall in demand had been greater it would have.

The strategies Clockwise can employ to deal with the rise in exchange rate are:

- Clockwise can use effective marketing techniques to strengthen the Clockwise brand image. This reduces the price elasticity of demand for the watches by making consumers more loyal to the Clockwise brand. With a more inelastic demand, any increase in price will actually increase revenue rather than reducing it after the increase. However, this would mean increasing expenditure on advertising and promotion which would be an added indirect expense.
- Clockwise could adopt a flexible pricing strategy where it reduces the price of the watches to foreign buyers when the value of sterling increases. However, this would cause a fall in the company's profit margin which would reduce their profitability.
- Clockwise could accept payment for the products it sells in the currency of the country it sells them in. For example, it could accept payment in French Francs. However, the company would lose out when they went to convert the currency into Sterling.

Conclusion

There is no easy way to deal with the problem of changes in the exchange rate that cause the price of the final product sold by Clockwise to change. It is important that the company keeps its brands strong so that it will maintain sales even when its prices increase and it is also important that it keeps price flexibility so that it can reduce prices when the exchange rate appreciates.

GLOBAL COMPETITION

Student book pages 274–275

1 The developing world has the following production advantages over the developed world:

- Workers in developing countries are paid much lower wages than those in the developed world which means the costs of production in the developing world are much lower. For example, labour in China is paid $1 per hour compared to $17 per hour in the US and $24 per hour in Germany.
- Generally speaking the working conditions are much lower in developing countries than they are in developed ones. This means that the cost of employing people in somewhere like Mexico is much lower than in the USA because the Mexican firm does not have to adhere to the same health and safety standards.
- The cost of land is lower in developing countries compared to developed countries. This makes it much cheaper for firms in the developing world to set up production.

2 As developing countries experience economic growth the incomes of the people who live in those countries rises. As their incomes rise they will have the funds to buy more goods and services, many of which are produced by companies in the UK. In a country like Mexico, for example, people will buy TVs, fridges, cars and designer clothing as their incomes rise. This is why a company like Nike has done so well marketing its products in developing countries. Because the growth in these countries has been so rapid, and because they have been relatively unexploited up to now, the potential for sales growth by UK firms in these countries is huge.

3 A computer manufacturer will be faced with the threat of cheap competition from developing countries. Producers in countries like Mexico, China and India are able to produce at lower unit cost because of the plentiful supply of cheap, skilled labour they have access to. To try and overcome this competition a computer manufacturer could adopt the following strategy:

- The company will need to keep its own unit costs down by increasing its productivity. This can be done by investing the latest technology, allowing workers to increase their output. The manufacturer will need to purchase the most up to date machinery used in the production of computers.
- The company will need to look at its production methods and organisation of workers. By employing team working and total quality management the productivity of the workforce could be increased and unit costs reduced.
- The quality of the product needs to be improved as a way of competing with low cost competition. This would mean redesigning the product and marketing it in a way that makes it different from the new competition. The new technology used in production, as well as the new production techniques used will help to improve the quality of the product the company produces.
- Finally, the computer company should look at targeting its product at market segments that are not as exposed to the low cost foreign competition. This could be in specialist areas where the quality of the product is important, and where a lot after sales service is needed.

The development of countries like China, Mexico and India will also offer the computer manufacturer significant opportunities that it can exploit:

- The company could look to buy in low cost components that it had originally made itself. This would reduce its direct costs of production. It could even produce some of its computers in these countries to allow it to market a low cost product that can compete more effectively on world markets.
- As developing countries grow the demand for computers will increase in their markets. The computer manufacturer should look to market their products in these countries to take advantage of the rising demand for computers.
- It is important that the computer manufacturer does not stand still, because it will see the demand for its products competed away by cheap new competition. It must take action to compete effectively in its traditional markets and also branch out to take advantage of the newly growing markets in the developing countries.

UNIT 10: The business environment – Section D: The influence of government

DIFFICULT TRADING CONDITIONS FOR HEA LTD

Student book pages 287–288

1 a Fiscal policy is the use of tax and government expenditure by the government to achieve its macroeconomic objectives. An expansionary fiscal policy which might be used to stimulate economic growth involves reducing tax and increasing government expenditure to try and raise demand in the economy and encourage economic growth. A tight fiscal policy that could be used to reduce inflation would involve raising tax and cutting government expenditure to reduce demand in the economy.

Monetary policy involves the manipulation of the supply of money using interest rates and credit controls to achieve economic objectives. An expansionary monetary policy to encourage economic growth would involve reducing interest rates to stimulate demand in the economy. A tight monetary policy used to reduce inflation involves the increase in interest rates to reduce demand.

b When monetary and fiscal policy are tightened, interest rates are increased, government expenditure is reduced and tax is increased. This leads to a fall in demand as the economy falls. As demand in the economy falls, businesses, like HEA, will experience a fall in the demand for their products. With lower demand businesses find it more difficult to sell their products which means they have to reduce their prices to remain competitive. As firms reduce their prices to keep competitive, the rate of inflation falls.

2 a A tightening in fiscal policy will have the following affects on HEA:

- The company's sales will fall as lower demand in the economy means that people spend less on designer clothes. The demand for designer clothes is quite responsive to changes in income because they are a luxury product, so there may well be a marked downturn in the demand for HEA's clothes.
- If direct tax is increased, the workers at HEA will have to pay more tax. This may lead to a reduction in their motivation and efficiency at work and they may also demand higher wages to make up for the reduction in their wages.
- If there is an increase in indirect tax HEA may be forced to increase its prices. This would certainly be the case if VAT was increased.
- If corporation tax is increased, it would mean that HEA's after tax profits would be reduced, which in turn cuts the amount it can pay in dividends and/or retain in the company.

A tight monetary policy will have the following effects on HEA:

- The company will experience a fall in sales as demand in the economy falls.
- HEA has a high proportion of borrowed funds used to finance it. A rise in interest rates will increase the cost of its finance.
- As sales fall and costs are increased, HEA's profits will fall.

HEA will be particularly hard hit by the rise in interest rates that has occurred. This is because the company has such a large proportion of borrowed finance. The company will also suffer because the demand for designer closing is a luxury product and responsive to changes in consumer incomes.

b HEA's stores in Canterbury and London have a large proportion of tourists as their customers. The tight monetary policy employed by the government will cause the value of the Pound to rise, which will make the UK a more expensive country for tourists to visit. With fewer tourists, the numbers of customers in the London and Canterbury stores will fall. The tourists who do visit the store will find that the higher value of the Pound will make the clothes that HEA is selling much more expensive.

3

Report on how HEA should deal with the problems caused by the tightening of monetary and fiscal policy by the UK Government

To: The directors of HEA

Objectives

To suggest how HEA can deal with the problem of a tightening in monetary and fiscal policy by considering:

- how it could change its marketing mix to maintain its sales
- how it can control its costs to maintain its profit margins
- change its finance to keep its interests cost down.

Strategy: marketing

- **Pricing:** to reduce the impact of falling demand on sales, HEA should put a discounting scheme in place. This would involve reducing the prices of slow moving lines, offering two for the price of one deals and offering coupons for money off the next purchase.
- **Promotion:** to support the pricing strategy, HEA should use extensive advertising in the local press to publicise the offers it is making.

Strategy: cost control

The scheme of discounts will lead to a reduction in profit margins. Thus it is important that costs in other areas are held down to allow the lower prices and keep some margin. This could be done by HEA pushing for lower prices from its suppliers. It could also change the way that employees are paid by increasing the proportion of their salary that is commission based. This would mean the staff would have to push products more forcefully and if the sales targets are not met the wage bill will fall.

Strategy: finance

As interest rates have increased, it is important for HEA to reduce the proportion of its funds that are borrowed. This may mean using owners capital to pay off some of their borrowed funds. The reduced borrowing costs will mean that HEA will have further scope to keep itself price competitive.

Conclusion

It is important that HEA uses the pricing, cost cutting and financing methods suggested, but does not compromise the things that have made the company successful. The change in the way its sales staff are paid is probably the most contentious proposal and this must be sold to the staff very carefully.

THE GOVERNMENT BUDGET AFFECTS HEALSTROME LTD

Student book pages 288–289

1 Healstrome has forecast that the sales of its picture frames will rise for the following reasons:

- The reduction in income tax means that consumers will have more disposable income which will increase their demand for goods and services. WH Smith and Athena will experience a rise in demand and will sell more picture frames, and this means a rise in demand for Healstrome's picture frames.
- The reduction in interest rates by the Bank of England means that people will have to pay less interest on their mortgages and other borrowing which will increase their demand for goods and services. This will again lead to a rise in the sales of picture frames from Healstrome.

b When a worker is employed, National Insurance is a tax paid partly by an employee and partly by the employer. If the employer's contribution to national insurance is reduced then it will mean that the wage cost of Healstrome will fall, which in turn reduces Healstrome's direct costs of production.

2 Healstrome's revised budgeted profit and loss account for 1999

	1999 original forecast £m	1999 new forecast £m
sales	22.50 × 1.03 × 1.04	24.10
cost of goods sold	8.20 × 0.98	8.04
gross profit	14.30	16.06
operating expenses	3.10	3.10
net profit	11.20	12.96
interest	1.20	1.00
profit before tax	10.00	11.96
tax	30% 2.7	32% 3.83
profit after tax	7.30	8.13
dividends	3.20	3.20
retained profit	4.10	4.93

Table 33 A revised budgeted profit and loss account for Healstrome

3 The short term benefits of a reduction in corporation tax will be:

- Healstrome will make a larger profit after tax, which means that it will be able to pay more dividends to its shareholders and or retain more profit within the business.
- The company's shareholders will be happier with a higher dividend payment and the extra retained profit can be used to fund more investment.

In the longer term:

- The higher dividend payments will mean that Healstrome will become a more attractive proposition for shareholders and will be able to raise more funds from this source.
- If Healstrome is able to retain more funds within the business which can be used to fund new investment then the company's long term profitability can be increased.

UNIT 10

The business environment – Section E: The impact of the law

PLAYRIGHT TOYS MAKES REDUNDANCIES

Student book page 296

1 Colin Edwards would need to take the following factors into account when making the necessary redundancies:

- The role of the contract of employment and what type of contract these workers were on. The contract would set out how much notice the employees would be given when they were made redundant and whether they would have any rights to redundancy payments.
- The length of service of the employees will be important because it will determine what redundancy payments they should be paid. The payment is calculated on the seniority of the employees and the length of time they have worked for the company.
- The company will also need to consider whether they will offer employees voluntary redundancy where workers can opt to take redundancy.

2 a The contract of employment is between an employee and the company that employs them. The contract offered by Playright Toys should include the following:

- a job description of the work the employee will undertake
- the pay
- the hours of work
- the holidays
- the pension rights
- the disciplinary rules and grievance procedure
- the length of notice given on resignation or termination

b A short term contract is different from a normal contract in that the short term contract will be terminated after a set time period; a new one will have to be negotiated if the employer and the employee want to continue their relationship. The new employees taken on by Playright will be employed on short term contracts.

c Playright Toys will gain the following advantages from employing the new workers on short term contracts:

- It will give Playright the flexibility to react to changes in demand for their products. If demand rises new employees can be taken on, and if it falls the company can easily lay staff off.
- There are fewer regulations governing the rights of employees with a short term contract which reduce employment costs.
- The company will be able to motivate the staff who will want their contract renewed.
- If an employee is not particularly good at their job then it will be easy for Playright to replace them.

However, there are the following disadvantages associated with short term contracts:

- Motivation of staff who do not identify with the Playright as much as people who are on long term contracts.
- Short term contracts lead to high staff turnover which leads to problems with team building within the organisation and the development of stable relationships with customers.
- Playright will have the additional cost of continuously renegotiating short term contracts.

- Playright will struggle to keep its employees when there is a shortage of workers in the labour market.

3 Playright could present the ideas for the employment changes that are going to take place in the following way:

- **Method of communication:** this can be done through meetings and consultations which involves the labour force. Communication is important because the workers need to feel they have some input into the decision making process. If the communication of the decision is made by letter or in the form of a notice after the decision has been taken it will be more difficult for the management to introduce the changes without the resistance of the trade union.
- **Content of communication:** the content of the communication needs to set out why the changes need to be made and the workforce need to understand the reasons and see the benefits of the changes. By doing this, the workforce is more likely to co-operate with the changes and for them to go through successfully.
- **Incentives:** to successfully introduce the changes a package of monetary and non monetary incentives would need be put together by Playright. This could involve generous redundancy packages for the redundant workers, as well as a higher salaries for the remaining workers.

Whilst it is necessary to get the workforce on the side of management when introducing the changes it will prove difficult because of the nature of the changes. If Playright wants to get the changes through they must have a strategy for dealing with any conflict that might arise.

PIZZA VILLAGE BURNS AN EMPLOYEE

Student book pages 296–297

1 a The Health and Safety Acts are designed to protect workers against accidents that happen in the work place. It is the employers responsibility under the Health and Safety at Work Act to 'ensure that they safeguard all their employees' health, safety and welfare at work'. The Act sets out the employer's responsibility to provide and maintain safety equipment and clothing, as well as the protection of employees against dangerous substances, such as hot fat. Pizza Village must safeguard their employees' health and safety as 'far as it is reasonably possible.' The Employees at Pizza Village also have a responsibility under the Health and Safety Act to act in a manner which takes reasonable responsibility for their own and other people's safety.

b Pizza Village's adherence to the Health and Safety at Work Act could be questioned on the following points:

- An employee has picked up a frying pan without using the gloves needed to protect their hands.
- The employee who dropped the frying pan claimed that he had not been given guidance on wearing protective gloves.
- The employee who dropped the frying pan claimed that he had been given no training on the use of the fryer.
- The employee who dropped the frying pan claimed that there were not enough protective gloves available.

To discover whether Pizza Village followed the Act properly, the employee's claims would need to be investigated. It may well have been the case that the employee had not followed the guidelines set by Pizza

Village and had not taken sufficient responsibility for their own and other people's health and safety.

2 a The principle of vicarious liability states that when an employee is carrying out work for an organisation, a situation may arise where the employee carries out a wrongful act. When this happens, the injured party can seek redress from the employees' employer. Through the principle of vicarious liability, Pizza Village may have to take responsibility for the actions of their employee who spilled the fat that injured another employee.

b The principle of vicarious liability means that Pizza Village would be liable to pay the costs of an action against an employee of the company when a wrongful act has been committed by the employee when doing their job of work. This could be very costly to Pizza Village in a situation like the one in the case study. If the injured employee was awarded a large amount of compensation for the injury they received it could have an impact on the company's finance. If Pizza Village does not take action to guard against such situations it could prove to be very expensive for the company if these types of events keep re-occuring.

c Pizza Village could take the following actions to protect themselves against vicarious liability:

- They could organise insurance to cover accidents that occur at work.
- They need to set up effective training for employees.
- Clear guidelines need to be given to employees about the use of equipment.
- Protective equipment must be made available.
- There needs to be effective management in the work place to guard against such situations.

Accidents like the spilling of the fat are less likely to occur if such courses of action are followed.

3 There are a number of pieces of legislation that have been set up to protect employees against discrimination at work. The Sex Discrimination Act, Race Relations Act and Equal Pay Act are all part of legislation to provide employees with equal opportunities at work. All employees should have an equal chance of being employed, or promoted, whatever their sex race, colour, religion or disability. The worker who wrote the letter about Health and Safety at Pizza Village said that he had been passed over for promotion at the company twice when women had been promoted ahead of him. If this man had been discriminated against, he would have a case against Pizza Village under the Sex Discrimination Act.

4 There are a number of advantages to Pizza Village of the existence of employment laws:

- The law as an enabler: A law like the minimum wage in the UK of £3.60 can work to the advantage of Pizza Village because competitors cannot reduce wages to exploititively low levels to gain a competitive advantage.
- If employees feel they are protected effectively at work by health and safety legislation, a minimum wage and equal opportunities, then this can raise staff morale and motivation in the organisation.

However, there are a number of disadvantages associated with employment laws:

- Extensive health and safety legislation and a minimum wage can significantly push up Pizza Villages costs. For example a minimum wage may mean that workers who are paid less than this have to have their wages increased. This will mean that other workers who are paid around £3.60 will also demand a wage increase to maintain their differentials with the lower paid workers.

- Extensive employment legislation reduces the flexibility of an organisation like Pizza Village. The whole decision making process is slowed down by rules and regulations that have to be followed. For example, all the rules governing termination of contracts, such as the payment of redundancy, means that businesses are reluctant to take on new staff because of the difficulty of getting rid of them.

The answer to the question of whether the employment laws are an advantage or disadvantage to Pizza Village will be found by looking at how protective they are of their employees as a point of principle. If the company do look after employees in terms of equal opportunities, pay and conditions then the regulations will have little negative impact on them. The regulations will have a positive impact on Pizza Village; they will gain a new competitive advantage as firms who did not follow regulations all that closely are forced to, and as a result lose their previous competitive advantage over Pizza Village.

UNIT 11

Employer–Employee relations

YARROW WORKERS VOTE FOR ACTION OVER 2% PAY OFFER

Student book pages 306–307

1 Industrial action is the method of activity used by a trade union to try and gets its way in an industrial dispute. The Yarrow workers used the following methods of industrial action in their dispute with the company

- **Overtime bans:** where workers refuse to do any overtime during a dispute.
- **Work to rule:** where workers stick precisely to the rules and regulations associated with their jobs. For example, a rule might state that five people are needed for a specific task and if only four are available the workers will refuse to do the job.
- **Strikes:** where workers refuse to work.

2 **a** Collective bargaining is where one or more trade unions negotiate on behalf of a whole group of workers at a work place, as opposed to workers negotiating on an individual basis with management. In the case of Yarrow, the GMB general union represents the interests of a group at workers at the company and negotiates on their behalf the 2% pay offer.
b Collective bargaining has the following advantages:

- In the collective bargaining process workers are organised into groups and form close group relationships. The formation of groups may make the workers at Yarrow more effective in their work as they develop greater cohesion and a feeling of belonging. The work of Elton Mayo showed through the Hawthorne Studies how important this is.
- The process of negotiation at Yarrow can be made more effective because it is simpler for management to talk with one body that represents the workforce rather than a large number of individual workers.
- Collective bargaining provides a focal point for workers to express their views which will come across clearly to management. Yarrow will know exactly what the view of the workforce are through collective bargaining.

The disadvantages of collective bargaining are:

- A powerful trade union with a leadership that has its own political agenda may use the collective workforce in conflict with management. The GMB union at Yarrow might use the workforce to achieve their own political objectives.
- Collective bargaining can force wages up beyond the level that the company can afford which leads to a rise in costs and a fall in profits. Through collective bargaining the GMB union could prevent changes at Yarrow which are necessary for the company's survival.

Collective bargaining has a number of advantages within the workplace in terms of communication and developing group strength. However, the union must act responsibly for their role within the organisation to help Yarrow as a company.

3 **a** Performance related pay is the use of pay to reward an employee's performance in their particular job. For example, if the workforce at Yarrow achieve a certain level of productivity then they will receive a bonus or an incentive payment. Performance related pay is used to try and improve the performance of workers.

b The GMB are concerned about the introduction of performance related pay for the following reasons:

- Performance related pay will mean that workers doing the same job will earn different wages. The GMB will be against this because their philosophy as a union will be to achieve the same decent wage for all their members.
- With performance related pay workers are more likely to work towards their own objectives and less likely to act collectively which may weaken the position of the GMB.
- Performance related pay means that the worker's performance has to be measured for the wage level to be set. It may not be easy to measure the performance of workers and they will lose out as a result of this. For example, workers on the production line at Yarrow might have their output limited by the speed of machinery.

4 **a** If there is a sustained period of industrial conflict Yarrow will experience the following problems:

- Production will become inefficient as workers work to rule and have overtime bans. This would increase the Yarrow's costs of production.
- If there is a dispute then the supply of ships produced by Yarrow will be interrupted which will let down the business's customers. This will mean that sales will be lost and revenue and profits will fall.

- As Yarrows's supply is interrupted and sales fall, Yarrow's cashflow position will deteriorate as a result of this.
- Industrial action will harm the reputation of Yarrow as a company and will reduce the prospects of future sales for the company. It may also make it difficult for the company to obtain future finance through a share issue or through borrowing.
- Industrial action will lead to a fall in morale at Yarrow. As workers are in dispute with management, many effective working relationships will be harmed and the degree of trust and respect between workers and management will be reduced.

An industrial dispute for Yarrow is going to be harmful in the short term as the sales and cashflow of the organisation are reduced, and in the long term the company's reputation will be damaged.

b The GMB union will face the following problems as a result of the industrial at Yarrow:

- If Yarrow runs into trouble because of the dispute and sales fall which leads to redundancies, then union members will lose their jobs and the power of the union at Yarrow will fall. Ultimately, Yarrow could fail which would be disastrous for the GMB union.
- If morale falls at Yarrow as a result of the dispute it could lead to splits between different groups within the union which will reduce the union's power.
- If the union is defeated in the dispute then it will lose power at Yarrow, and its reputation throughout the company will be adversely affected.

EMPLOYER–EMPLOYEE RELATIONS

5

Report on how industrial action at the Yarrow Shipbuilders can be avoided

To: The Directors at Yarrow Shipbuilders

Objectives

- To suggest a strategy for avoiding an industrial dispute at Yarrow.
- To suggest how management should communicate with the workforce.
- To suggest how the management could persuade the workforce to accept the new working practices.
- To suggest how arbitration could be used to help resolve any disputes that take place.

Method

- **Communication:** it is important that the workforce at Yarrow are clear about the direction the company is going in. The management should explain the reasons behind the decisions to the whole workforce in a series of meetings. It should be made clear that the future success of the company is dependent on the changes in working practices taking place. It is also important that the workers are invited to give their own contributions on how the changes should be introduced, so that they feel they have had a part in the decision making process.
- The workers should be given genuine **financial incentives** to go over to the new working practices. The pay offer might need to be increased and some concessions made on working conditions. Management should be seen to give some lead in the process of change by themselves putting into practice changes to improve performance.
- It is important that the company offers **a plan for arbitration** to make sure that dispute is avoided at all costs. This would involve the use of ACAS as an arbitration service to provide a solution to the dispute.

Conclusion

It is vital that Yarrow's management introduces the changes that need to take place without a damaging industrial dispute. This is most likely to occur with the support and the co-operation of the workforce. For this reason, the workforce must be given some say in the introduction of the new working practices.

A SHOCK FOR JAGUAR

Student book pages 307–308

1 a The Transport and General Workers Union (TGWU) is a general union that represents workers in different industries with different skills. The TGWU represents workers at Jaguar and also workers in other industries such as airlines.

b By negotiating with workforce through the TGWU Jaguar will gain the following advantages:

- The process of negotiation at Jaguar can be made more effective because it is simpler for management to talk with one body that represents the workforce rather than a large number of individual workers. By talking to the whole workforce through collective bargaining Jaguar is able to forge a single agreement which can be applied to the entire workforce. Negotiating with workers on an individual basis will be much more time consuming.

- Negotiations on an individual basis could lead to workers obtaining different rates of pay for the same job. This situation could lead to disharmony amongst the workforce.
- Collective bargaining provides a focal point for workers to express their views on a number of issues which will come across clearly to management. Jaguar will know exactly what the views of the workforce are through collective bargaining.

However collective bargaining can lead to the following problems:

- Jaguar's workforce could, through collective bargaining, push wages up beyond the level that Jaguar can afford. This will leads to a rise in costs, a fall in profits and if prices have to be increased by the company a fall in sales, which, in the long term, could lead to Jaguar making workers redundant.
- Through collective bargaining a powerful trade union could use the collective workforce in conflict with management. However, in the case study the workers went against the advice of the TGWU to accept the pay offer, suggesting that the TGWU were not taking the workforce on a path to conflict.
- In certain situations, a collective agreement may not be to Jaguar's advantage; when a single agreement means that workers are paid the same wage it may not allow for differences in skills, or demand conditions that mean workers should earn different pay levels. For example a national wage agreement may not take into account the differing cost of living that exists between regions, which means that different wage rates should be paid in different regions.

Collective bargaining is useful to both Jaguar and its workers in term of saving time and resources, but it must be applied responsibly by both parties to be effective.

2 **a** The Jaguar workers rejected the pay deal because they would have to work compulsory overtime on top of their basic 37 hour work. The workers may have their working week extended without them having any choice. If they had to work 50 hours to meet production targets then they would have no choice. The compulsory overtime could mean that workers would be made redundant and their work would be done through overtime. If the demand for Jaguar cars increased, Jaguar could have held down the workforce putting increased pressure on the existing workers.

b If there was a breakdown in negotiations the dispute could have led to an industrial dispute and the following consequences for Jaguar:

- Their output of cars would be lost which would lead to lower sales and profits.
- Jaguar would lose market share as customers went to other companies such as BMW for their cars. These customers could be lost in the long term if they felt happy with their new choice of car.
- Jaguar's reputation would have been damaged by conflict which could have reduced its long term sales and made it more difficult for the company to raise funds through the stock market.
- An industrial dispute would adversely affect morale at Jaguar and lead to a deterioration of the relationship between the workforce and management. Less effective management would adversely affect the performance of the company.

The workforce would have suffered the following consequences from an industrial dispute:

- If there was a strike, workers would suffer a loss of income because they would not be paid.
- There would be a loss of morale and a breakdown of good relations with management if there was a strike. The

working conditions at Jaguar would deteriorate in the short term at least.
- There could be divisions between individual workers who agreed or did not agree with a strike. This could again cause morale to fall at Jaguar.
- If the future prospects of the company were harmed by an industrial dispute, then this could lead to lower wages and redundancies for the workforce in the future.

In both the short and long term it is clear that the workforce, company management, and Jaguar company itself will lose if there is a strike. Thus it is imperative that a fair solution is found to avoid a strike.

3 The Advisory Conciliation and Arbitration Service (ACAS) could be used to find a solution at Jaguar. ACAS will intervene if one or more of the parties in the dispute invites them, although its involvement must be agreed by both parties. ACAS would look at evidence from both side of the dispute and be asked to make a ruling which is binding on both parties. If ACAS found that the offer made by Jaguar was a fair one, but that the compulsory overtime should be left of the agreement, then both parties would have to accept the ruling.

4 When calling a strike the TGWU must follow the trade union legislation passed in the 1980s. This states that the union must hold a secret ballot of all its members involved in the dispute to see whether they are in favour of a strike.

5

Report on how the new working practices can be introduced at Jaguar with industrial action being avoided

To: The Directors at Jaguar

Objectives

- To suggest a strategy for introducing new working practices at Jaguar avoiding an industrial dispute.
- To suggest how management should communicate with the workforce.
- To suggest how the management could persuade the workforce to accept the new working practices.
- To suggest how arbitration could be used to help resolve any disputes that take place.

Method

- **Communication:** it is important that the workforce at Jaguar are clear about the direction the company is going in. Jaguar's management should explain clearly the reasons behind the decisions to whole workforce in a series of meetings. It should be made clear that the future success of the company is dependent on the changes in working practices taking place. It is also important that the workers are invited to give their own contributions on how the changes should be introduced, so that they feel they have had a part in the decision making process. The work of Elton Mayo and Douglas Mcgregor demonstrated how important it is to involve the workforce in the decision making process to introduce change successfully.
- The workers should be given genuine **financial incentives** to go over to the new working practices. This would be advocated by Taylor and Mcgregor's Theory Y manager. The pay offer might need to be increased and some concessions made on overtime working. Management should be seen to give some lead in the process of change by themselves putting into practice changes to improve performance.

- It is important that Jaguar offers **a plan for arbitration** to make sure that the dispute is avoided at all costs. This would involve the use of ACAS as an arbitration service to provide a solution to the dispute.

Conclusion

It is to promote Jaguar's success in the short and long term that its management introduces the changes that need to take place without a damaging industrial dispute. By gaining the support and the co-operation of the workforce, the introduction of new working practices is much more likely to be successful. It is critical that the workforce must be given some say in the introduction of the new working practices.

LOW MORALE IN HOSPITAL

Student book pages 303–309

1 a The British Medical Association (BMA) is a professional association that represents the interests of doctors. It puts forward the views of doctors on issues that affect them like pay, working conditions, health care funding, disciplinary matters and general medical practice. Unlike a trade union, the BMA would not call for industrial action.

b The BMA could be useful to the management of the NHS trust because it will provide them with views that are representative of doctors who are vital in the implementation of the management's decisions. For example, the successful implementation of changes in the way that waiting lists are managed would have to have the co-operation of doctors, and the BMA would be able to put forward their collective view.

The BMA could hinder the management's decision making by using their power to make it difficult for management to implement their decisions. Doctors will have one perspective on the way that a hospital should be run which fits with their own interests and perhaps not the hospital's interest. Through publicity the BMA could make it difficult for management to implement their decision.

2 a The ancillary staff could take the following industrial action:

- **Overtime bans:** where workers refuse to do any overtime during a dispute.
- **Work to rule:** where workers stick precisely to the rules and regulations associated with their jobs. For example, a rule might state that two porters are needed to move a patient and if only one porter is available the patient would not be moved.
- **Strikes:** where workers refuse to work.

b The Trust management could try to resolve the dispute in the following ways:

- Through negotiation the ancillary staff and management could come to a compromise agreement which avoids the dispute.
- The dispute could be taken to arbitration where the Advisory Conciliation and Arbitration Service (ACAS) is brought in to resolve the dispute. If both sides agree to using ACAS, any solution brought about by ACAS would be binding on both parties.

3 The key motivational problems facing the NHS trust are:

- There is a problem with excess workload which is affecting doctors and nurses. The increase in workload has been generated by changes to the way the NHS is organised. Workload would be identified by Hertzberg as a maintenance factor which, when it fails to satisfy the worker, acts as a demotivating factor. The stress caused by excess workload affects the security of the employee which, in terms of Maslow's hierarchy of needs, inhibits the workers' movement to higher levels of the hierarchy and reduces their motivation at work.
- Under pay is a demotivating factor. If workers feel that they are not being valued highly enough through remuneration their motivation will fall. Pay is a maintenance factor identified by Hertzberg which, when it is not satisfied, acts as a demotivator. The management theorist F.W. Taylor would also argue that low levels of pay would be a demotivating factor.
- Doctors and nurses who have been set demanding targets to achieve when there is a shortage of resources will become demotivated. This is made worse by workers feeling that they are unable to achieve the targets they are set by the government.

The increasingly pressured conditions that hospital workers experience, together with a level of pay that they feel does not represent what they deserve, combine to create a low level of motivation within the hospital.

b

Report on how motivation of staff within the health service can be improved

To: The Managers of the Queen Mary II NHS Trust

Objectives

- to suggest how the level of staff motivation within the Queen Mary II NHS Trust can be improved
- to talk to the staff about how conditions can be improved
- to see how the workload of staff could be made more manageable
- to deal with the problem of low pay
- funding the changes.

Strategy

- **Communication:** it is vital that the management at the hospital are consulted fully through a series of meetings about how motivation can be improved. This would involve taking on board the suggestions of the staff about how things can be improved.
- **Workload:** to raise the level of staff motivation it is critical that the work load of staff is made more manageable. It is important that management introduces systems that help reduce staff workload. There will have to be an increase in the number of staff that work in the hospital so that the amount of work can be spread out amongst more people.
- **Pay:** this is a difficult issue because the pay of health service staff is negotiated at a national level which make it impossible for the Trust to increase pay. However, the award of incentive payments and grades can be used to see how changes to the staff's pay can be improved.
- **Funding:** to reduce workload, employ more staff and pay those staff more will need more funding. The Trust could try to reduce waste and inefficiency and ways of achieving this to save money should be found. The Trust will need to go to the Government to try and increase the funds it is given. The Trust could look for funding outside government sources to

provide it with money. This could come from selling certain services, such as beds in private rooms.

Conclusion

The problem of improving staff motivation in the Queen Mary II Hospital is a difficult one because it ultimately requires an increase in funding, which tightly controlled by the government.

However, action needs to be taken by management to:

- involve doctors and nurses in decision making
- reduce the workload of staff through reorganisation of systems and more effective management
- to try and improve pay levels
- to try and increase funding to allow the changes to take place.

4 There are the following arguments against the management of the Health service accepting the pay increase of 15%:

- If the managers accept the pay award it will have a negative affect on their relationship with doctors and nurses who have only been awarded 4%. The award will mean that morale amongst this group of workers is bound to sink even lower and make any attempt to raise motivation much more difficult.
- The position of management in the dispute involving ancillary staff will be more difficult to resolve if the managers have just received a 15% pay award. There is more likely to be a strike which will cost the hospital money, reduce morale and reduce the hospital's performance further.
- The pay award to management will mean that there is less money available to the Trust when funds are already very tight. Money used to pay managers could been used to recruit new staff to help over-worked nurses.

However, if the management accept the offer it will:

- Help motivate management who are under considerable pressure in that it is an extremely difficult management task. To improve conditions in the hospital well motivated managers are needed.
- If the pay increase is paid it will mean that the Trust can retain managers who might leave for other jobs in the private sector. A high turnover of managers would be a further problem for the hospital.
- The pay increase will help to attract new, talented managers to the hospital. Talented managers are more likely to solve the problems of the hospital.

In the short term, the acceptance of the pay award by the managers may be extremely damaging for the hospital because of the impact it will have on the morale of other staff. However, the long term performance of the hospital can possibly only be improved by more effective managers who need to be attracted by good salary levels.